Affirmative
Action

POINT COUNTERPOINT

Affirmative Action

Alan Marzilli

SERIES CONSULTING EDITOR
Alan Marzilli, M.A., J.D.

CHELSEA HOUSE
PUBLISHERS

A Haights Cross Communications Company

Philadelphia

CHELSEA HOUSE PUBLISHERS

VP, NEW PRODUCT DEVELOPMENT   Sally Cheney
DIRECTOR OF PRODUCTION   Kim Shinners
CREATIVE MANAGER   Takeshi Takahashi
MANUFACTURING MANAGER   Diann Grasse

Staff for AFFIRMATIVE ACTION

EXECUTIVE EDITOR   Lee Marcott
SENIOR EDITOR   Tara Koellhoffer
PRODUCTION EDITOR   Megan Emery
ASSISTANT PHOTO EDITOR   Noelle Nardone
SERIES AND COVER DESIGNER   Keith Trego
LAYOUT   21st Century Publishing and Communications, Inc.

A Haights Cross Communications ⚡ Company

http://www.chelseahouse.com

First Printing

1 3 5 7 9 8 6 4 2

Library of Congress Cataloging-in-Publication Data

Marzilli, Alan.
   Affirmative action/by Alan Marzilli.
      p. cm.—(Point/counterpoint)
Includes index.
   ISBN 0-7910-7918-X
   1. Affirmative action programs—Juvenile literature. [1. Affirmative action
programs.] I. Title. II. Point-counterpoint (Philadelphia, Pa.)
HF5549.5.A34M267 2004
331.13'3'0973—dc22

                                                          2003023903

CONTENTS

Introduction

Alan Marzilli, M.A., J.D.
Durham, North Carolina

The debates presented in POINT/COUNTERPOINT are among the most interesting and controversial in contemporary American society, but studying them is more than an academic activity. They affect every citizen; they are the issues that today's leaders debate and tomorrow's will decide. The reader may one day play a central role in resolving them.

Why study both sides of the debate? It's possible that the reader will not yet have formed any opinion at all on the subject of this volume—but this is unlikely. It is more likely that the reader will already hold an opinion, probably a strong one, and very probably one formed without full exposure to the arguments of the other side. It is rare to hear an argument presented in a balanced way, and it is easy to form an opinion on too little information; these books will help to fill in the informational gaps that can never be avoided. More important, though, is the practical function of the series: Skillful argumentation requires a thorough knowledge of *both* sides—though there are seldom only two, and only by knowing what an opponent is likely to assert can one form an articulate response.

Perhaps more important is that listening to the other side sometimes helps one to see an opponent's arguments in a more human way. For example, Sister Helen Prejean, one of the nation's most visible opponents of capital punishment, has been deeply affected by her interactions with the families of murder victims. Seeing the families' grief and pain, she understands much better why people support the death penalty, and she is able to carry out her advocacy with a greater sensitivity to the needs and beliefs of those who do not agree with her. Her relativism, in turn, lends credibility to her work. Dismissing the other side of the argument as totally without merit can be too easy—it is far more useful to understand the nature of the controversy and the reasons *why* the issue defies resolution.

The most controversial issues of all are often those that center on a constitutional right. The Bill of Rights—the first ten amendments to the U.S. Constitution—spells out some of the most fundamental rights that distinguish the governmental system of the United States from those that allow fewer (or other) freedoms. But the sparsely worded document is open to interpretation, and clauses of only a few words are often at the heart of national debates. The Bill of Rights was meant to protect individual liberties; but the needs of some individuals clash with those of society as a whole, and when this happens someone has to decide where to draw the line. Thus the Constitution becomes a battleground between the rights of individuals to do as they please and the responsibility of the government to protect its citizens. The First Amendment's guarantee of "freedom of speech," for example, leads to a number of difficult questions. Some forms of expression, such as burning an American flag, lead to public outrage—but nevertheless are said to be protected by the First Amendment. Other types of expression that most people find objectionable, such as sexually explicit material involving children, are not protected because they are considered harmful. The question is not only where to draw the line, but how to do this without infringing on the personal liberties on which the United States was built.

The Bill of Rights raises many other questions about individual rights and the societal "good." Is a prayer before a high school football game an "establishment of religion" prohibited by the First Amendment? Does the Second Amendment's promise of "the right to bear arms" include concealed handguns? Is stopping and frisking someone standing on a corner known to be frequented by drug dealers a form of "unreasonable search and seizure" in violation of the Fourth Amendment? Although the nine-member U.S. Supreme Court has the ultimate authority in interpreting the Constitution, its answers do not always satisfy the public. When a group of nine people—sometimes by a five-to-four vote—makes a decision that affects the lives of hundreds of millions, public outcry can be expected. And the composition of the Court does change over time, so even a landmark decision is not guaranteed to stand forever. The limits of constitutional protection are always in flux.

These issues make headlines, divide courts, and decide elections. They are the questions most worthy of national debate, and this series aims to cover them as thoroughly as possible. Each volume sets out some of the key arguments surrounding a particular issue, even some views that most people consider extreme or radical—but presents a balanced perspective on the issue. Excerpts from the relevant laws and judicial opinions and references to central concepts, source material, and advocacy groups help the reader to explore the issues even further and to read "the letter of the law" just as the legislatures and the courts have established it.

It may seem that some debates—such as those over capital punishment and abortion, debates with a strong moral component—will never be resolved. But American history offers numerous examples of controversies that once seemed insurmountable but now are effectively settled, even if only on the surface. Abolitionists met with widespread resistance to their efforts to end slavery, and the controversy over that issue threatened to cleave the nation in two; but today public debate over the merits of slavery would be unthinkable, though racial inequalities still plague the nation. Similarly unthinkable at one time was suffrage for women and minorities, but this is now a matter of course. Distributing information about contraception once was a crime. Societies change, and attitudes change, and new questions of social justice are raised constantly while the old ones fade into irrelevancy.

Whatever the root of the controversy, the books in POINT/ COUNTERPOINT seek to explain to the reader the origins of the debate, the current state of the law, and the arguments on both sides. The goal of the series is to inform the reader about the issues facing not only American politicians, but all of the nation's citizens, and to encourage the reader to become more actively involved in resolving these debates, as a voter, a concerned citizen, a journalist, an activist, or an elected official. Democracy is based on education, and every voice counts—so every opinion must be an informed one.

———————●———————————●—————————●———————

Should universities, employers, and government agencies give preferences to people based on their race? This important question came before the U.S. Supreme Court in June 2003 in two separate cases involving affirmative action programs at the University of Michigan. Many people thought that the Court might strike down affirmative action programs across the board. Instead, the Court struck down one of the university's affirmative action programs, but let another stand. The difference was that the acceptable plan gave individualized attention to each applicant and considered many factors other than race. Civil rights activists hailed the latter decision as a victory for racial equality, but at the same time, voters in several key states have eliminated affirmative action at the state level. This book examines the University of Michigan decisions in-depth, as well as the other key issues in the affirmative action debate at the state level.

Affirmative Action and the University of Michigan Cases

During the summer of 1963, a few hundred thousand people from across the nation gathered in Washington, D.C., to rally for the civil rights of African Americans. It was a protest against the many indignities suffered by African Americans, including being forced to attend separate schools, being turned away from motels and restaurants, and being denied opportunities for good jobs and a college education. From the steps of the Lincoln Memorial, the Reverend Dr. Martin Luther King, Jr., delivered what would become perhaps the most famous civil rights speech in American history: "I have a dream that my four little children will one day live in a nation where they will not be judged by the color of their skin but by the content of their character." [1]

In the late 1960s, state governments engaged in systematic discrimination against minorities, with governors of Southern states clinging to the idea of segregation despite the U.S. Supreme Court's ruling that keeping apart the races in schools and other public places violated the Constitution. Thanks to the dedication of activists like King, and a federal government determined to prosecute violations of civil rights, local and state governments slowly abandoned their segregationist policies. However, prejudice still survived in the hearts of many people in control of the nation's most powerful institutions, like governments, banks, labor unions, universities, businesses, and even places of worship.

The Origin of Affirmative Action Policies

In an effort to combat discrimination against African Americans in the 1960s, the administration of President Lyndon B. Johnson introduced an entirely new concept. The president recognized that merely prohibiting discrimination was not enough to level the playing field: The effects of centuries of segregation and legalized discrimination had put African Americans at a severe disadvantage. They had attended inferior schools, had been barred from good jobs, and had been shut out of the political process. President Johnson's administration therefore proposed that "affirmative action" be taken to ensure that minorities received jobs, promotions, admission to universities, and other important opportunities.

> • **Should people expect a "level playing field" in life? Should race be an obstacle?**

To Martin Luther King, the idea of discrimination was so repugnant that he hoped for a day when people would not be judged by the color of their skin, yet affirmative action policies actively and openly take race into account. The difference is that the goal is to *help* African Americans and other minorities who have historically been the victims of government-sponsored discrimination. King dreamed of a day when his children would be judged without their race being taken into consideration.

But he understood the role of affirmative action in the meta-morphosis of the United States into a "color-blind" nation, because underlying prejudice and the disadvantages faced by minorities were simply too great to ignore.

More than three decades after King's speech, the federal government, most state governments, and many businesses, schools, and universities continued to use affirmative action policies. Sometimes these policies have been limited to extra efforts to recruit minority candidates, but frequently, affirmative action policies have favored hiring, promoting, or admitting minority candidates who—at least on paper—seem less qualified than nonminority candidates who are rejected. For example, a university might admit African-American or Hispanic students whose grade point averages (GPAs) and standardized test scores are much lower than those of white candidates who are denied admission. In some fields—like police and fire depart-ments—affirmative action policies might include women. Typically, Asian Americans are not considered "minorities" for university affirmative action programs, so university admission programs largely target African Americans, Hispanics, and Native Americans.

> • **Have you experienced discrimination? Have you benefited from affirmative action?**

Affirmative Action or "Reverse Discrimination"?

Is it fair to extend preferences to select minority groups? Certainly during the 1960s, African Americans faced the greatest level of hatred and discrimination from entrenched white institutions, and Hispanics have suffered tremendously as well. But isn't there also a history of discrimination against women, Asian Americans, Catholics, Jews, Italian Americans, Irish Americans, and other groups? The argument typically advanced against extending affirmative action to these groups is that they are already well represented in the workforce and in higher education. The goal—many proponents of affirmative action say—is no longer to remedy past discrimination per se, but to increase the diversity of America's workforce, government, and universities. African Americans, Hispanics, and Native Americans—perhaps in large part because of past and present discrimination—are largely underrepresented in positions of power and influence in the United States. To supporters of affirmative action, King's dream is still a long way off.

However, the flip side of affirmative action is that many people who do not benefit from such programs feel they have become the victims of "reverse discrimination"—that in the same way laws once favored whites over African Americans, the laws now favor minorities and women over white males. Opponents think that preferences favoring race over merit are outdated and that the time for a "color-blind" society is now. The states of California, Texas, and Florida, for example, have passed laws eliminating the consideration of race in decisions like admissions to state universities.

Although racism persists in American society, government-sponsored discrimination against minorities has been illegal for many years. But ending legalized discrimination was a slow process. The Fourteenth Amendment to the U.S. Constitution, ratified at the end of the Civil War after slavery was abolished, prohibits states from denying people "the equal protection of the laws." The purpose of this 1868 amendment was to prohibit states, especially Southern states where slavery had been legal, from passing laws that treated African Americans as inferior. Yet the states were defiant, and for more than a century, so-called Jim Crow laws that segregated public facilities blatantly treated African-American citizens differently. In the last few decades, such laws have disappeared, but affirmative action policies have remained in effect as the only type of government policies that make distinctions according to race. Many people believe that the time to end *all* discrimination has come.

The University of Michigan Cases

One person calling for an end to "reverse discrimination" is Jennifer Gratz. Described by the *Washington Post* as a "blond homecoming queen from a blue-collar family" in suburban Detroit "with stellar grades . . . and good looks to boot," she dreamed of attending college at the University of Michigan, the state's nationally renowned public university in Ann Arbor.[2] She applied in 1995; at the time, the college used a system that placed applicants into a table based on GPA and test scores. The applicant's location in the table determined if he or she would be admitted, rejected, or delayed ("wait-listed"). An applicant to the University of Michigan with Gratz's GPA of 3.8 and her score on the American College Test (ACT) of 25 out of 36 would have been accepted—if that applicant was African-American, Hispanic, or Native American.

However, Jennifer Gratz was white, and her location in the table put her on an extended wait-list; she eventually enrolled in another college when she realized she would not be able to attend the University of Michigan. As she told *NewsHour With Jim Lehrer*, a national news program, "I believe I was racially discriminated against, and that's wrong."[3] She decided to take legal action against the university, and with the help of a conservative public interest law firm in Washington, D.C., her case eventually made it to the U.S. Supreme Court. Before Gratz's case was heard by the Supreme Court, the university had changed its undergraduate admissions policies several times. Eventually, it settled on a system in which all applicants were ranked on a scale from 0 to 150. Anyone scoring above 100 would be admitted, and below that were point ranges that would determine if an applicant would be admitted, admitted later, wait-listed, or rejected. African Americans, Hispanics, and Native Americans automatically received twenty points on the scale, a mechanism to help the school increase the diversity of its student body.

- **Should test scores and grades be the most important factor in college admissions?**

Barbara Grutter, who is also white, had an experience similar to Gratz's when she applied to the University of Michigan Law School in 1996. She had a GPA in college of 3.8 and a Law School Admission Test (LSAT) score of 161 out of 180. Many people with similar (or lower) numbers were admitted, including minorities. However, unlike the college, the law school did not automatically award points to people based on their race. Instead, as described by the U.S. Supreme Court:

> The [law school's] policy requires admissions officials to evaluate each applicant based on all the information available in the file, including a personal statement, letters of recommendation, and an essay describing the ways in which the applicant will contribute to the life and diversity of the law school. . . . In reviewing an applicant's file, admissions officials must consider the applicant's undergraduate grade point average (GPA) and Law School Admission Test (LSAT) score because they are important (if imperfect) predictors of academic success in law school. . . .
>
> The policy requires admissions officials to look beyond grades and test scores to other criteria that are important to the law school's educational objectives. . . . So-called "'soft' variables" such as "the enthusiasm of recommenders, the quality of the undergraduate institution, the quality of the applicant's essay, and the areas and difficulty of undergraduate course selection" are all brought to bear in assessing an "applicant's likely contributions to the intellectual and social life of the institution." . . .
>
> The policy aspires to "achieve that diversity which has the potential to enrich everyone's education and thus make a law school class stronger than the sum of its parts." . . . The policy does not restrict the types of diversity contributions eligible for "substantial weight" in the admissions process, but instead recognizes "many possible bases for diversity admissions." . . . The policy does, however, reaffirm the law school's longstanding commitment to "one particular type of diversity," that is, "racial and ethnic diversity with special reference to the inclusion of

students from groups which have been historically discriminated against, like African Americans, Hispanics and Native Americans, who without this commitment might not be represented in our student body in meaningful numbers." . . . By enrolling a "'critical mass' of [underrepresented] minority students," the law school seeks to "ensur[e] their ability to make unique contributions to the character of the law school."[4]

Both Jennifer Gratz and Barbara Grutter appeared on paper to be much stronger candidates than many people who were admitted to the University of Michigan's undergraduate college and law school. But in the interest of increasing the number of minority students, the university accepted minority applicants with lower grades and test scores than Gratz's and Grutter's. The major difference between the two systems was that the undergraduate college automatically awarded points to people based on their race, while the law school considered race as one of many factors. This distinction would become significant as the cases made their way to the U.S. Supreme Court.

> • **Do the college and law school systems seem to be significantly different?**

In a surprise move, the Supreme Court ruled on Gratz's and Grutter's lawsuits on the same day in June 2003, but reached opposite conclusions. By a 6–3 vote, the Court struck down the undergraduate college's admission policy, which automatically awarded twenty points to underrepresented minorities. The Court held that the policy violated Gratz's and others' guarantee of "equal protection of the laws" under the Constitution. But the Court, in a 5–4 vote, upheld the law school's efforts to increase the diversity of its student body by considering race alongside other factors. In effect, the *Grutter* decision validated the opinion of Justice Lewis F. Powell, Jr., writing for himself twenty-five years earlier in *Regents of the University of California v. Bakke,* in which he stated: "[T]he attainment of a diverse

Supreme Court upholds affirmative action

Universities are allowed to give minority applicants an edge in the admissions process, but race cannot be the determining factor, the Supreme Court ruled in two separate decisions.

	Gratz v. Bollinger	Grutter v. Bollinger
Plaintiff	Jennifer Gratz and Patrick Hamacher, both students rejected from the university's Ann Arbor campus	Barbara Grutter, rejected from the Law School
Defendant	University of Michigan's College of Literature, Science and the Arts	University of Michigan Law School
Lawsuit	Filed in October 1997, the plaintiffs charged that the point-based system used by the admissions office, which automatically gave minorities one-fifth of the points needed to guarantee admission, violated the 1964 Civil Rights Act	Filed in December 1997, Grutter made a similar charge challenging the law school's race-based admissions, which was less-structured than the point system used for undergraduates
Ruling	Voted 6-3 to strike down the undergraduate admission's point system because it was "not narrowly tailored to achieve the interest in educational diversity."	Voted 5-4 to uphold the law school's affirmative action program saying "higher education must be accessible to all individuals."

SOURCES: Associated Press; The Center for Individual Rights   **AP**

The year 2003 was a landmark in affirmative action jurisprudence. The U.S. Supreme Court ruled on two related cases that set new precedents for how affirmative action may be applied in the future. This chart reviews the two lawsuits, known together as the University of Michigan cases.

student body . . . is a constitutionally permissible goal," so long as the "program treats each applicant as an individual in the admissions process."[5]

The Court's split decisions did little to quell the national debate on affirmative action. The Court held that diversity provides a proper rationale for affirmative action programs; however, any affirmative action program must consider factors other than race. The Court did not say that the Constitution prohibits *all* affirmative action programs, nor that the Constitution requires states to run such programs. Essentially, the Court answered the question "Are affirmative action programs acceptable?" with a resounding "maybe." Across the

FROM THE BENCH

Opinion of Justice Powell in *Bakke*

The fourth goal asserted by petitioner is the attainment of a diverse student body. This clearly is a constitutionally permissible goal for an institution of higher education. Academic freedom, though not a specifically enumerated constitutional right, long has been viewed as a special concern of the First Amendment. The freedom of a university to make its own judgments as to education includes the selection of its student body.... [T]he "nation's future depends upon leaders trained through wide exposure" to the ideas and mores of students as diverse as this nation of many peoples....

It may be assumed that the reservation of a specified number of seats in each class for individuals from the preferred ethnic groups would contribute to the attainment of considerable ethnic diversity in the student body. But petitioner's argument that this is the only effective means of serving the interest of diversity is seriously flawed. In a most fundamental sense the argument misconceives the nature of the state interest that would justify consideration of race or ethnic background. It is not an interest in simple ethnic diversity, in which a specified percentage of the student body is in effect guaranteed to be members of selected ethnic groups, with the remaining percentage an undifferentiated aggregation of students. The diversity that furthers a compelling state interest encompasses a far broader array of qualifications and characteristics of which racial or ethnic origin is but a single though important element. Petitioner's special admissions program, focused solely on ethnic diversity, would hinder rather than further attainment of genuine diversity.

An illuminating example is found in the Harvard College program:...

When the Committee on Admissions reviews...applicants who are "admissible" and deemed capable of doing good work in their courses, the race of an applicant may tip the balance in his favor just as geographic origin or a life spent on a farm may tip the balance in other candidates' cases. A farm boy from Idaho can bring something to Harvard College that a Bostonian cannot offer. Similarly, a nation, people are debating whether affirmative action programs should be abolished. States like California, Texas, Florida, and Washington have passed laws severely restricting or eliminating affirmative action plans. And the debate continues elsewhere: in corporations, universities, and statehouses across the country.

black student can usually bring something that a white person cannot offer. . . .

In such an admissions program, race or ethnic background may be deemed a "plus" in a particular applicant's file, yet it does not insulate the individual from comparison with all other candidates for the available seats. The file of a particular black applicant may be examined for his potential contribution to diversity without the factor of race being decisive when compared, for example, with that of an applicant identified as an Italian American if the latter is thought to exhibit qualities more likely to promote beneficial educational pluralism. Such qualities could include exceptional personal talents, unique work or service experience, leadership potential, maturity, demonstrated compassion, a history of overcoming disadvantage, ability to communicate with the poor, or other qualifications deemed important. In short, an admissions program operated in this way is flexible enough to consider all pertinent elements of diversity in light of the particular qualifications of each applicant, and to place them on the same footing for consideration, although not necessarily according them the same weight. Indeed, the weight attributed to a particular quality may vary from year to year depending upon the "mix" both of the student body and the applicants for the incoming class.

This kind of program treats each applicant as an individual in the admissions process. The applicant who loses out on the last available seat to another candidate receiving a "plus" on the basis of ethnic background will not have been foreclosed from all consideration for that seat simply because he was not the right color or had the wrong surname. It would mean only that his combined qualifications, which may have included similar nonobjective factors, did not outweigh those of the other applicant. His qualifications would have been weighed fairly and competitively, and he would have no basis to complain of unequal treatment under the Fourteenth Amendment.

From: *Regents of the University of California v. Bakke*, 438 U.S. 265 (1978) (Opinion of Powell, J.)

Since the 1960s, many states, universities, and employers have operated "affirmative action" programs to help minorities. The Supreme Court recently approved affirmative action programs that consider race as one of many factors, but several states have abolished their own affirmative action programs.

FROM THE BENCH

From *Gratz* v. *Bollinger*

Justice Powell's opinion in *Bakke* emphasized the importance of considering each particular applicant as an individual, assessing all of the qualities that individual possesses, and in turn, evaluating that individual's ability to contribute to the unique setting of higher education. The admissions program Justice Powell described, however, did not contemplate that any single characteristic automatically ensured a specific and identifiable contribution to a university's diversity.... Instead, under the approach Justice Powell described, each characteristic of a particular applicant was to be considered in assessing the applicant's entire application.

The current LSA [the University of Michigan College of Literature, Science, and the Arts] policy does not provide such individualized consideration. The LSA's policy automatically distributes twenty points to every single applicant from an "underrepresented minority" group, as defined by the university. The only consideration that accompanies this distribution of points is a factual review of an application to determine whether an individual is a member of one of these minority groups. Moreover, unlike Justice Powell's example, where the race of a "particular black applicant" could be considered without being decisive ... the LSA's automatic distribution of twenty points has the effect of making "the factor of race ... decisive" for virtually every minimally qualified underrepresented minority applicant....

Even if [a nonminority student's] "extraordinary artistic talent" rivaled that of Monet or Picasso, the applicant would receive, at most, five points under the LSA's system. . . . At the same time, every single underrepresented minority applicant ... would automatically receive twenty points for submitting an application. Clearly, the LSA's system does not offer applicants [an] individualized selection process....

Affirmative Action Is No Longer Justified as a Remedy for Racism

Affirmative action in the United States began during the 1960s. It was supposed to be a temporary measure to make up for widespread discrimination against African Americans and other minorities, but many people have started to wonder when it will end. In the *Grutter* decision, which upheld the University of Michigan Law School's consideration of an applicant's race in order to achieve a "critical mass" of underrepresented minorities, the Supreme Court also noted: "[All] government use of race must have a logical end point." The Court further predicted, "We expect that 25 years from now, the use of racial preferences will no longer be necessary. . . ."[1] But for many opponents of affirmative action, the time to stop the use of racial preferences has come; many people believe that the original justification for such programs—the endemic racism that foreclosed many opportunities to minorities during the 1960s—no longer provides a valid rationale for their continuation today.

Although opponents of affirmative action believe it is proper to take action against specific acts of discrimination, they do not agree that racial preferences are an answer to "societal discrimination." The problem, they say, is that not all members of a minority group have been the victims of specific acts of discrimination, and, therefore, racial preferences are much too broad a solution. Legally speaking, it has been a number of years since the Supreme Court has accepted past societal discrimination as a justification for affirmative action, but a majority of the Court has not definitively rejected the concept to the extent that some opponents of affirmative action would like.

In two cases involving the awarding of construction contracts to minority-owned businesses, the Court concluded that general societal discrimination did not justify preferential treatment for minority-owned businesses. For example,[2] the Court struck down a policy by the city of Richmond, Virginia, of giving preference to minority groups, including Aleutian Islanders, who hail from the coastal islands of Alaska. There was simply no evidence that anyone of Aleutian ancestry had ever tried to get a construction contract with the city, let alone been denied one due to racism. However, in these cases, the Court held that past discrimination in awarding contracts, if specifically proven, might provide a basis for racial preferences. If the city had discriminated against an Aleutian-owned construction company, presumably, the policy might have been upheld.

However, to Justice Antonin Scalia, it is not enough that other members of a racial group have been discriminated against. He would help the Aleutian-owned company that was the victim of discrimination but not other companies that had not suffered discriminatory treatment. In the second case, which invalidated contracts awarded by the federal government, Justice Scalia wrote a separate opinion to clarify his own belief that past discrimination could not be remedied by racial preferences: In his view, two wrongs do not make a right. He wrote:

> [A] government can never have a "compelling interest" in discriminating on the basis of race in order to "make up" for past racial discrimination in the opposite direction. . . . Individuals who have been wronged by unlawful racial discrimination should be made whole; but under our Constitution there can be no such thing as either a creditor or a debtor race. . . . To pursue the concept of racial entitlement— even for the most admirable and benign of purposes—is to reinforce and preserve for future mischief the way of thinking that produced race slavery, race privilege and race hatred. In the eyes of government, we are just one race here. It is American. [3]

However, Justice Scalia is still trying to persuade all of his colleagues to say definitively that past racism does not justify affirmative action.

> • **Is it wise to give preferences to all minority groups, or only to those who really need them?**

Many groups that have suffered from discrimination now succeed without preferences.

One main argument cited by opponents of affirmative action is that many groups have suffered—and continue to suffer— blatant discrimination in American society, and while only some of these groups benefit from affirmative action policies, members of other groups succeed without them. For example, during an era of steady immigration from Ireland, employers frequently hung signs reading, "Irish need not apply." During World War II, when the country was at war with Japan, the federal government rounded up innocent Japanese-American citizens and held them at camps. There are countless groups that have been the object of blatant societal discrimination in the past and continue to be the object of more subtle forms of

I agree with ...Justice O'Connor's conclusion that strict scrutiny must be applied to all governmental classification by race, whether or not its asserted purpose is "remedial" or "benign." ... I do not agree, however, with Justice O'Connor's dictum suggesting that, despite the Fourteenth Amendment, state and local governments may in some circumstances discriminate on the basis of race in order (in a broad sense) "to ameliorate the effects of past discrimination." ...

In my view there is only one circumstance in which the states may act by race to "undo the effects of past discrimination": where that is necessary to eliminate their own maintenance of a system of unlawful racial classification. If, for example, a state agency has a discriminatory pay scale compensating black employees in all positions at 20 percent less than their nonblack counterparts, it may assuredly promulgate an order raising the salaries of "all black employees" to eliminate the differential. ... This distinction explains our school desegregation cases, in which we have made plain that states and localities sometimes have an obligation to adopt race-conscious remedies. While there is no doubt that those cases have taken into account the continuing "effects" of previously mandated racial school assignment, we have held those effects to justify a race-conscious remedy only because we have concluded, in that context, that they perpetuate a "dual school system." ...

In the particular field of state contracting, for example, it may adopt a preference for small businesses, or even for new businesses—which would make it easier for those previously excluded by discrimination to enter the field. Such programs may well have racially disproportionate impact, but they are not based on race. And, of course, a state may "undo the effects of past discrimination" in the sense of giving the identified victim of state discrimination that which it wrongfully denied him—for example, giving to a previously rejected black applicant the job that, by reason of discrimination, had been awarded to a white applicant, even if this means terminating the latter's employment. In such a context, the white jobholder is not being selected for disadvantageous treatment because of his race, but because he was wrongfully awarded a job to prejudice today. Jews, Italian Americans, and people whose origins are from many countries—Korea, Poland, Pakistan, India, China, Vietnam, Russia—all endure bigotry in this country. Yet, none of these groups benefits from typical affirmative action policies.

which another is entitled. That is worlds apart from the system here, in which those to be disadvantaged are identified solely by race.

I agree with the court's dictum that a fundamental distinction must be drawn between the effects of "societal" discrimination and the effects of "identified" discrimination, and that the situation would be different if Richmond's plan were "tailored" to identify those particular bidders who "suffered from the effects of past discrimination by the city or prime contractors." . . . Nothing prevents Richmond from according a contracting preference to identified victims of discrimination. While most of the beneficiaries might be black, neither the beneficiaries nor those disadvantaged by the preference would be identified on the basis of their race.

It is plainly true that in our society blacks have suffered discrimination immeasurably greater than any directed at other racial groups. But those who believe that racial preferences can help to "even the score" display, and reinforce, a manner of thinking by race that was the source of the injustice and that will, if it endures within our society, be the source of more injustice still. The relevant proposition is not that it was blacks, or Jews, or Irish who were discriminated against, but that it was individual men and women, "created equal," who were discriminated against. And the relevant resolve is that that should never happen again. Racial preferences appear to "even the score" (in some small degree) only if one embraces the proposition that our society is appropriately viewed as divided into races, making it right that an injustice rendered in the past to a black man should be compensated for by discriminating against a white. Nothing is worth that embrace. Since blacks have been disproportionately disadvantaged by racial discrimination, any race-neutral remedial program aimed at the disadvantaged as such will have a disproportionately beneficial impact on blacks. Only such a program, and not one that operates on the basis of race, is in accord with the letter and the spirit of our Constitution.

From: *Richmond* v. *J.A. Croson Co.*, 488 U.S. 469 (Scalia, J., concurring in the judgment).

Conservative talk-show host Sean Hannity believes that even without racial preferences, the United States is a land of opportunity. He recalls meeting a man who had fled what was then Communist-controlled Czechoslovakia, a man "who had been deprived of liberties his entire life" and arrived in the United States with no money. The man started a small business cleaning office buildings and, within a few years, owned two houses. To Hannity, this man provided a perfect example of how a person can suffer from persecution, yet rise above it. Hannity laments that others do not seize the American Dream as this man did. He writes: "[Some people act] as if being given the *opportunity* to achieve is not enough. They act as though they expect material blessings to be bestowed upon them without any effort on their part. Some have bought into the lie that America is a racist, sexist, bigoted, homophobic country that keeps minorities down and does so intentionally." [4] Hannity believes that the United States provides ample opportunity for everyone.

> • **What is the difference between experiencing oppression in another country and experiencing oppression in the United States?**

Minority leaders are too quick to blame problems on racism.

Hannity is not alone in his belief that the impact of racism on opportunity is grossly overstated. Larry Elder, another conservative talk-show host, criticizes the "victicrat mentality" of many African-American leaders. Elder, who is African-American, writes in his book, *The Ten Things You Can't Say in America*, that racism did not stop him from achieving his goals, but that highly visible leaders often discourage young people by portraying society as a racist environment in which African Americans cannot succeed. He writes, "Imagine an inner-city child raised in a home without a father. . . . He attends a bad school; sees drug dealing around him [and] listens to gangsta rap. . . . 'Black leaders' tell him the white man intends to bring him down . . . that standardized tests like the SAT are culturally biased . . . [and] that he can't get into college without affirmative action. . . . At some point, this kid says to himself, 'Why bother?'"[5] Often, the belief that a person cannot succeed is a self-fulfilling prophecy that helps perpetuate the belief that racism makes achievement impossible: In Elder's example, the young man who gives up on academics ends up failing in life, only to blame racism for his problems.

Elder believes that, to the extent the "victicrat mentality" has discouraged achievement among African Americans, constant cries of racism have done more harm than good. The answer, he believes, is not affirmative action but hard work. In his book, he recalls a time when a friend took him to a library in midtown Los Angeles, where the population is primarily Asian-American and Hispanic. Outside the library, a group of Hispanic youths were riding skateboards, but inside the library, every chair was occupied by Korean-American youths and their parents. Despite the availability of affirmative action programs for Hispanics, Elder believes that the hard work of the Korean youths is better than any quota system. Elder ponders: "[Fast] forward ten or twenty years later. Which group will likely generate the senior vice president of sales and marketing[?] . . . The library shows affirmative action remains alive and well in our country. Only some call it homework."[6]

Innocent people suffer and undeserving people benefit from racial preferences.

A major source of criticism of using racial preferences to combat past discrimination is that such programs do not make any distinction between the guilty and the innocent, the deserving and the undeserving. The University of Michigan's undergraduate admission program struck down by *Gratz*, for example, awarded twenty points to every minority candidate.

By denying these twenty points to every white candidate, some would say, the system effectively "punished" these applicants, whether or not they had done anything wrong. Most teenagers applying to college are not themselves racist, and they certainly are not to blame for excluding African Americans from higher education or jobs. Why then, critics ask, should they be discriminated against in the admissions process? In the words of the conservative jurist Robert Bork, whose nomination to the Supreme Court was derailed by liberal groups: "It makes little sense, or justice, to sacrifice a white or a male who did not inflict discrimination to advance the interests of a black or a female who did not suffer discrimination. No old injustice is undone, but a new injustice is inflicted."[7]

Similarly, many affirmative action programs provide benefits

FROM THE BENCH

[T]he law school has no comparative advantage in measuring the present effects of discrimination in primary and secondary schools in Texas. Such a task becomes even more improbable where, as here, benefits are conferred upon students who attended out-of-state or private schools for such education. Such boundless "remedies" raise a constitutional concern beyond mere competence. In this situation, an inference is raised that the program was the result of racial social engineering rather [than] a desire to implement a remedy....

By the late 1960s, the school had implemented its first program designed to recruit minorities . . . and it now engages in an extensive minority recruiting program that includes a significant amount of scholarship money. The vast majority of the faculty, staff, and students at the law school had absolutely nothing to do with any discrimination that the law school practiced in the past.

In such a case, one cannot conclude that a hostile environment is the present effect of past discrimination. Any racial tension at the law school is most certainly the result of present societal discrimination, and if anything, is contributed to, rather than alleviated by, the overt and prevalent consideration of race in admissions.

Source: *Hopwood* v. *Texas*, 78 F.3d 932 (5th Cir. 1996).

to people who might not really need them. For example, affirmative action programs provide preferential treatment to people who belong to minority groups but come from wealthy, well-educated families. Many programs would favor an African-American applicant whose father is a successful businessman with a Harvard degree, while awarding no "bonus points" to a white applicant whose father had been a political prisoner in an oppressive Eastern European country. Perhaps more strikingly, affirmative action programs have been in use long enough so that a college applicant might benefit from racial preferences even though his or her parents had also benefited from such preferences. If the goal of affirmative action is to level the playing field, many wonder if it makes sense to give preferences to second-generation affirmative action beneficiaries.

In some cases, preferences in the name of "diversity" can even serve the purposes of favoritism and racial discrimination. With population shifts in recent decades, white people have become the minority in many cities, and as a result of voting patterns, many local governments are dominated by minorities. Though there is no real danger that these minority-dominated governments would discriminate against minority-owned businesses when awarding valuable city contracts, the cities have nonetheless maintained a system of giving preferential treatment to minority-owned businesses. Terry Eastland, the publisher of *The Weekly Standard*, writes, "With the advent . . . of minority-dominated governments, minorities have discriminated against nonminorities by fashioning affirmative action programs that . . . are little more than expressions of racial politics, the ignoble triumph of minority majorities."[8]

> • **What justifies the awarding of minority preferences by minority-dominated local governments? Is there any danger of discrimination against minorities without the preferences?**

Opponents of affirmative action have adopted Justice Scalia's belief that there cannot be "a creditor or a debtor race" because there is no way of reaching any conclusion about someone's character based simply on race. As the Asian American Legal Foundation argued in the University of Michigan cases:

> True diversity is a goal best pursued without recourse to race. It is simplistic to assume that any given African American candidate has suffered adversity and disadvantage, thereby gaining valuable perspective or experience, while assuming that the opposite is true for any given Chinese American candidate. Even where such a generalization could be made for a group as a whole, common sense tells us it would never be true for all individuals in the group.[9]

The conservative Claremont Institute was even more blunt in its argument in the University of Michigan cases, stating:

> [The] principles of the Declaration of Independence, codified at long last in the Constitution via the Fourteenth Amendment, will not countenance racial discrimination that purports to remedy past wrongs against individuals of one race by conferring benefits upon others who happen to share the same skin color, at the expense of those who do not. As Dr. King [said] that August day on the steps of the Lincoln Memorial, "In the process of gaining our rightful place . . . we must not be guilty of wrongful deeds."[10]

> • **Should a problem like racism be addressed head-on or swept under the rug?**

Because discrimination ultimately harms individuals within a minority group, but not necessarily all members, opponents of affirmative action believe that it is unfair to give preferential treatment to some groups, whose members might not all need help, while denying preferential treatment to other people who have suffered discrimination and other forms of adversity. In the words of U.S. Supreme Court Justice Antonin Scalia, the Constitution does not recognize "a creditor or a debtor race."

Racism Still Pervades Society

A young African-American man named Morrison told author and sociology professor Annie S. Barnes about attending a predominantly white university in Illinois when he was eighteen years old. One day, while discussing slavery during an American history class—in which he was the only African-American student—something happened that reminded him that racism is alive and well in the United States. According to his recollection, "[the instructor] showed a picture of Mammy, the well-known black stereotypical woman. . . . She weighed about 300 pounds with charcoal black skin, large exaggerated red lips, and an old familiar smile on her face like she was happy being a slave. . . . [A] white student, my age, yelled out that the Mammy picture looked like my mama."[1]

Supporters of affirmative action vigorously dispute claims

that racism has diminished to the point that affirmative action is no longer justified. In his essay "Ten Myths About Affirmative Action," psychology professor Scott Plous writes: "Despite the progress that has been made, the playing field is far from level. . . . Black people continue to have twice the unemployment rate of white people, twice the rate of infant mortality, and just over half the proportion of people who attend four years or more of college. . . . In fact, without affirmative action the percentage of blacks at many selective schools would drop to only 2 percent of the student body. . . ."[2] Minorities suffer great disparities in wealth, employment, and access to the justice system, and Plous and others believe that affirmative action is needed to combat the racism that helps to cause these disparities.

Supporters of affirmative action say opponents' claims that "reverse discrimination" has harmed thousands of innocent whites are untrue; novelist and journalist Anna Quindlen calls such claims "The Great White Myth." She writes, "Listen [to white opponents of affirmative action] and you will believe that the construction sites, the precinct houses, [and] the investment banks are filled with African Americans. Unless you actually visit them."[3] Law professors Charles R. Lawrence III and Mari J. Matsuda call the claim that racism has ended "the big lie": "To believe [that white males have become innocent victims of reverse discrimination] we must accept a formal and extremely narrow definition of racial discrimination or racism, under which only self-professed bigots are racists and none of us is held responsible for perpetuating the white supremacy of even the very distant past."[4] Quindlen, Lawrence, Matsuda, and many others believe that American society still has far to go before the effects of discrimination are overcome.

- **Do overall numbers do anything to appease someone who feels like a victim of "reverse discrimination"?**

Affirmative action is needed to overcome economic injustice.

A major thrust of affirmative action programs has been to reduce widespread poverty among minorities. Although opponents have tried to say that racial preferences should be replaced with standards that take only poverty and social class into account, supporters of affirmative action programs believe that race still "matters." Many civil rights leaders believe that poverty, unemployment, low education levels, and other major societal problems facing African Americans are the direct result of racism, both official racism practiced by the government and the racism of white Americans. In the University of Michigan Law School case,

FROM THE BENCH

Educational institutions, the court acknowledges, are not barred from any and all consideration of race when making admissions decisions.... But the court once again maintains that the same standard of review controls judicial inspection of all official race classifications.... This insistence on "consistency," ... would be fitting were our nation free of the vestiges of rank discrimination long reinforced by law.... But we are not far distant from an overtly discriminatory past, and the effects of centuries of law-sanctioned inequality remain painfully evident in our communities and schools.

In the wake "of a system of racial caste only recently ended," ... large disparities endure. Unemployment, poverty, and access to health care vary disproportionately by race. Neighborhoods and schools remain racially divided. African-American and Hispanic children are all too often educated in poverty-stricken and under-performing institutions. Adult African Americans and Hispanics generally earn less than whites with equivalent levels of education. Equally credentialed job applicants receive different receptions depending on their race. Irrational prejudice is still encountered in real estate markets and consumer transactions. "Bias both conscious and unconscious, reflecting traditional and unexamined habits of thought, keeps up barriers that must come down if equal opportunity and nondiscrimination are ever genuinely to become this country's law and practice."...

The Constitution instructs all who act for the government that they may not "deny to any person ... the equal protection of the laws." ... In implementing the National Association for the Advancement of Colored People (NAACP) and the American Civil Liberties Union (ACLU) argued:

> More than 300 years of slavery, segregation, and invidious discrimination by public and private actors have produced a systemic racial hierarchy that continues to this day. Numerous studies document continuing widespread racial inequality in virtually every aspect of our society, including education, employment, income, housing, health care, life expectancy, criminal justice, and in the accumulation of wealth. . . . In short, race matters, significantly—not because it should, but because it does.[5]

this equality instruction, as I see it, government decisionmakers may properly distinguish between policies of exclusion and inclusion. . . . Actions designed to burden groups long denied full citizenship stature are not sensibly ranked with measures taken to hasten the day when entrenched discrimination and its after-effects have been extirpated. . . .

The stain of generations of racial oppression is still visible in our society . . . and the determination to hasten its removal remains vital. One can reasonably anticipate, therefore, that colleges and universities will seek to maintain their minority enrollment—and the networks and opportunities thereby opened to minority graduates—whether or not they can do so in full candor through adoption of affirmative action plans of the kind here at issue. Without recourse to such plans, institutions of higher education may resort to camouflage. For example, schools may encourage applicants to write of their cultural traditions in the essays they submit, or to indicate whether English is their second language. Seeking to improve their chances for admission, applicants may highlight the minority group associations to which they belong, or the Hispanic surnames of their mothers or grandparents. In turn, teachers' recommendations may emphasize who a student is as much as what he or she has accomplished. . . . If honesty is the best policy, surely Michigan's accurately described, fully disclosed college affirmative action program is preferable to achieving similar numbers through winks, nods, and disguises.

From *Gratz* v. *Bollinger* (Ginsburg, J., dissenting)

- **Is slavery still relevant to the discussion of affirmative action? Does it make a difference *why* someone came to the United States?**

Well after the abolition of slavery, government policies discriminated against African Americans, a form of "economic injustice" that, even today, has left a vastly disproportionate number of African Americans and other minorities living in poverty. A problem frequently cited by civil rights leaders is that minorities tend to live in segregated neighborhoods, in which almost all residents are of the same race, and in which poverty tends to be rampant. As described by the NAACP and ACLU:

> Starting with the New Deal, "federal housing policies translated private discrimination into public policy" and officially endorsed the discriminatory practices of real estate developers, banks, mortgage brokers, appraisers, and insurance agents. Blacks were confined to overcrowded, overpriced, and deteriorating "ghettos" whose inferior services included inadequate, segregated schools. Many black communities were completely isolated by an iron curtain . . . on all sides, which created massive overcrowding, a "race tax" on housing prices, and deterioration of housing within predominantly black neighborhoods. The sorry legacy of these policies persists long after the enactment of fair housing laws, as fears of the "black ghetto" contribute to racial discrimination and flight from integrated neighborhoods.[6]

Although conservative opponents of affirmative action like to tell anecdotes about immigrants arriving in the United States and making their own fortunes, supporters say that such individual success stories are not representative of the bleak prospects faced by many of America's poor. The stark reality is that too many Americans, especially minorities, grow up in poverty without access to a quality education. As Democratic political consultant James Carville noted, "Most immigrants came to the United States for opportunity for themselves. But let's face it, blacks originally came to this country to provide opportunity for [white] planters. . . . [For] a lot of blacks today, their greatest opportunities are to be harassed by a cop . . . to go hungry when they're young, to attend inferior schools, and to get thrown in prison. Not exactly the kind of opportunity America is supposed to be built on."[7]

The United Negro College Fund (UNCF), which had its origins in helping minorities obtain college educations in an era when they were barred from many universities, has argued that affirmative action in education is the means for overcoming economic injustice. In the University of Michigan cases, the group wrote:

> [E]ducation is a particularly important means of overcoming past racial discrimination. Education opportunity provides not only the means for individual success . . . but also a way to lessen the underlying prejudices that burden historically disfavored groups. . . . The education of African Americans and other minorities also is important to the nation's general welfare. It is well documented that, over a lifetime, a college graduate will earn nearly double the income of a high school graduate. . . . One cannot underestimate the value added to America when she educates her minority citizens.[8]

In the view of the United Negro College Fund, affirmative action in college admissions is not just about where people attend college, but about the economic future of minorities.

Affirmative action is needed to combat workplace discrimination.

Currently, many public and private employers operate affirmative action programs in which they give special consideration to minorities. These can take the form of hiring preferences, special efforts to recruit minorities, and even internship programs designed exclusively for minorities. Why should employers use affirmative action programs when there are many laws against discrimination? Supporters say that so-called equal opportunity laws are broken constantly, as employers silently discriminate in hiring, pay scales, job duties, promotions, and firing. Because catching discrimination is so difficult, they argue, affirmative action is necessary.

Annie S. Barnes's book *Everyday Racism* chronicles the racism that African Americans face daily in the United States. In a chapter on employment discrimination, Barnes tells of a woman, Lucerne, who saw a help-wanted sign in a store window and, having two years of experience in retail, asked the manager for a job application. The manager hesitated before giving her the application and would not interview her, even though nobody was shopping there at the time. What happened next is unfortunately all too typical, according to Barnes: "Lucerne called back a few days later. The manager told Lucerne that the position had been filled. Yet the Help Needed sign was still in the window. Lucerne asked a white friend to inquire about the job. The friend reported that she was told they were still hiring."[9]

The numbers back up Barnes's conclusions: Studies show that minorities have a more difficult time finding jobs than whites do. In the University of Michigan cases, the nation's largest labor organization, the American Federation of Labor–Congress of Industrial Organizations (AFL-CIO) cited an unpublished study, "Are Emily and Brendan More Employable Than Lakisha and Jamal?", which demonstrated scientifically the job discrimination faced by minorities. Researchers at the University of Chicago and the Massachusetts Institute of Technology sent out thousands of fake résumés in response to real job advertisements. For each job, they sent multiple résumés offering similar qualifications but different names. Résumés with "white-sounding" names generated calls for about one out of every ten jobs, but the résumés with names popular among African Americans received calls only about one out of every fifteen times.[10]

- **What does a study using fake résumés tell us about employment patterns?**

The only way to address such discrimination, the AFL-CIO suggests, is to use affirmative action policies that encourage the hiring of minority job applicants. Laws prohibiting racial discrimination are not enough because employers will simply act on their own prejudices, finding excuses not to hire minority job seekers. In its brief to the Supreme Court, the AFL-CIO argued:

> While the primary aim of [the federal employment discrimination law] Title VII was to eliminate discrimination in hiring, research reveals that such discrimination persists and is the least susceptible to legal sanction. . . . [A]bsent express exclusionary policies, most applicants who are discriminated against in hiring never know it. . . . Two primary causes of employment discrimination, particularly in hiring, are stereotypes and prejudice arising out of the physical separation of people of differing races and ethnic groups that exists in our society.[11]

FROM THE BENCH

Having approved the use of race as a factor in the admissions process, the majority proceeds to nullify the essential safeguard [of] rigorous judicial review, with strict scrutiny as the controlling standard. . . . This court has reaffirmed, subsequent to *Bakke*, the absolute necessity of strict scrutiny when the state uses race as an operative category. . . . The court confuses deference to a university's definition of its educational objective with deference to the implementation of this goal. In the context of university admissions the objective of racial diversity can be accepted based on empirical data known to us, but deference is not to be given with respect to the methods by which it is pursued. Preferment by race, when resorted to by the state, can be the most divisive of all policies, containing within it the potential to destroy confidence in the Constitution and in the idea of equality. The majority today refuses to be faithful to the settled principle of strict review designed to reflect these concerns.

From *Grutter* v. *Bollinger* (Kennedy, J., dissenting)

Affirmative action is needed to combat racism in the justice system.

The Supreme Court's ruling in the University of Michigan Law School case was destined to have an impact far beyond the university or university education in general: The case also would help to determine the face of American justice. Many people believe that the court system is biased against minorities. Although lynching has all but disappeared, minorities in many communities are still not likely to receive a fair trial when accused of a crime. Minority defendants are more likely to be convicted and receive harsher sentences. African Americans convicted of murder are much more likely than white defendants to receive death sentences, especially when their victims are white. Even in civil cases, like property disputes, many people perceive that minorities face a disadvantage in accessing the court system.

A frequent explanation for disparities in the court system is the lack of minority judges. For example, a group of Black Law Student Associations (BLSA) from elite law schools argued in the *Grutter* case:

> The racial composition of the judiciary represents a significant factor in the public's estimation of whether judges will dispense justice fairly. . . . [A] 1999 study revealed a perception among many citizens, including 68 percent of blacks, that the judicial system treats blacks unfavorably compared to whites. . . . Notably, 43 percent of whites and 42 percent of Hispanics surveyed agreed that blacks are treated less favorably than whites in the courts.[12]

According to the Hispanic National Bar Association (HNBA), minorities account for only about 6 percent of all federal judges. Some people argue that increasing the number of minority lawyers, and especially judges, would help balance the system's inequities. As the HNBA said in the *Grutter* case, "Enhanced diversity in the legal profession will reduce racial and ethnic bias by promoting equal access to justice and real racial and ethnic equity."[13] Many people believe that minority judges will be more fair in criminal trials and will support reforms in accessing the court system.

Attending law school is a necessary step that people must take to become lawyers, and, therefore, judges. Groups like the BLSAs and the HNBA support affirmative action because they believe it is the only reliable mechanism to ensure that minorities attend law school in numbers sufficient to make the court system more representative of the nation's diversity. In the Michigan case, the groups argued that abolishing affirmative action would lower the number of minority law school graduates, as shown by the low number of minorities who attended law school before affirmative action and the decreasing numbers of students who attend law schools in states that have banned affirmative action. Although the University of Michigan's system was upheld, some groups are concerned that the increasing number of law schools that have abandoned affirmative action programs will further increase the racial imbalance in judgeships.

- **Do you think that the justice system is fair?**

Supporters of affirmative action say that race still matters in a very significant way. Minorities face poverty, job discrimination, and a biased court system. Supporters say that affirmative action policies are needed to help to correct these and other injustices.

Efforts to Promote "Diversity" Harm Society

I n the University of Michigan cases, the university's policy was to extend preferences to groups that have historically been the victims of discrimination—African Americans, Hispanics, and Native Americans. Although a desire to remedy past discrimination might have influenced the decision by university administrators to enact this policy, the university's stated justification was to increase "diversity" on campus.

The law school sought to have a "critical mass" of minority students in each class. This term is borrowed from nuclear physics, in which critical mass is the amount of radioactive material needed to cause a chain reaction. In the context of law school admissions, critical mass means the number of minority students needed to establish a community and a comfort level in the classroom. Opponents of affirmative action, however, think that tampering with the admissions process to admit a minimum number of minorities is like playing with explosives.

The benefits of "diversity" are unproven.

The promotion of affirmative action programs as a way of achieving diversity gained momentum with Justice Lewis F. Powell, Jr.'s opinion in the 1978 *Regents of the University of California* v. *Bakke* decision. The case invalidated the "quota systems" at one of the University of California medical schools, which reserved a set number of seats in each class for under-represented minorities. The Court was divided 4–4, but Powell bridged the competing blocs. Writing for himself, rather than the Court as a whole, Justice Powell suggested that, although strict quotas are invalid (as one bloc maintained), the "attainment of a diverse student body" provided a justification for affirmative action that was consistent with the U.S. Constitution's equal protection clause (siding with the other bloc). In the years that followed, many universities, employers, and government agencies began to promote their affirmative action policies as tools for increasing diversity. Although Justice Powell's "solo" opinion could not be considered the law of the land, affirmative action supporters latched onto his words.

> • **Is there a real difference between quota systems and using race as a "plus" factor?**

In the months leading up to the Supreme Court's considera-tion of the University of Michigan cases, opponents of affirmative action worked actively to dissuade the Court from accepting the "diversity" justification of affirmative action. One problem, they said, is that once diversity is accepted as a rationale for affirmative action, the groups to which preferences might be extended are almost limitless. For example, to increase diversity, a university might decide to extend preferences to people who have had sex-change operations. Though opponents of affirmative action certainly would not like to see the use of preferences expanded, they also believe that diversity is a flawed rationale even as it is used today—primarily to extend preferences to African Americans, Native Americans, and Hispanics.

The full Supreme Court gave Justice Powell's words the force of law by upholding diversity as a justification for the University of Michigan Law School's affirmative action policy in *Grutter*. By that time, paradoxically, the University of California—which was the subject of the *Bakke* decision—had been operating for

FROM THE BENCH

The "educational benefit" that the University of Michigan seeks to achieve by racial discrimination consists, according to the court, of "cross-racial understanding," and "better prepar[ation of] students for an increasingly diverse workforce and society,"...all of which is necessary not only for work, but also for good "citizenship." ...This is not, of course, an "educational benefit" on which students will be graded on their law school transcript (Works and Plays Well with Others: B+) or tested by the bar examiners (Q: Describe in 500 words or less your cross-racial understanding). For it is a lesson of life rather than law—essentially the same lesson taught to (or rather learned by, for it cannot be "taught" in the usual sense) people three feet shorter and twenty years younger than the full-grown adults at the University of Michigan Law School, in institutions ranging from Boy Scout troops to public-school kindergartens. If properly considered an "educational benefit" at all, it is surely not one that is either uniquely relevant to law school or uniquely "teachable" in a formal educational setting. And therefore: If it is appropriate for the University of Michigan Law School to use racial discrimination for the purpose of putting together a "critical mass" that will convey generic lessons in socialization and good citizenship, surely it is no less appropriate—indeed, particularly appropriate—for the civil service system of the State of Michigan to do so. There, also, those exposed to "critical masses" of certain races will presumably become better Americans, better Michiganders, better civil servants. And surely private employers cannot be criticized—indeed, should be praised—if they also "teach" good citizenship to their adult employees through a patriotic, all-American system of racial discrimination in hiring. The nonminority individuals who are deprived of a legal education, a civil service job, or any job at all by reason of their skin color will surely understand.

From *Grutter* v. *Bollinger* (Scalia, J., concurring in part and dissenting in part)

several years without an affirmative action policy. In 1996, California voters enacted a law that barred state universities from using racial preferences. Opponents of affirmative action elsewhere think that the diversity rationale should be abandoned nationally, as it has been in California; many believe that diversity is merely a facade. In *Ending Affirmative Action*, Terry Eastland writes: "The founding rationale of affirmative action was to remedy the ill effects of past discrimination against blacks, but this rationale did not easily fit the other groups. So affirmative action was redefined and rejustified in terms of overcoming 'underrepresentation' and achieving 'diversity.'"[1]

The primary objection is that while diversity might seem like a desirable outcome, there is not enough evidence that it has any benefits other than diversity for its own sake. And opponents feel that it is certainly not a desirable enough outcome to justify what they see as "reverse discrimination." Sociologist Frederick Lynch interviewed a number of business executives for his book, *The Diversity Machine*. Though companies have spent untold millions on affirmative action programs and cultural sensitivity training, Lynch suggests that such programs do not actually benefit businesses. He writes, "A glaring dilemma for proponents of workforce diversity programs has been the lack of systematic social science evidence that the programs deliver the promised results of increased productivity, and improved intergroup relations."[2]

- **Can you explain why diversity might be desirable?**

The University of Michigan contended that racial diversity within the student body results in a diversity of viewpoints in the classroom. But many people disputed the claim that the only way to achieve a diversity of viewpoints was to artificially create racial diversity through preferential admission policies. Many objected by saying that because every person thinks differently, there is no reason to assume that minority students think differently from white students. A group of conservative law professors wrote in the *Grutter* case:

Racial diversity is not required to foster a full discussion of issues and viewpoints in the classroom. If a white applicant and a black applicant each have the same view on an issue . . . there is no true "intellectual" or "academic" reason for admitting one of the students over the other. . . .

[The university] hardly needs racial preferences to teach the obvious—that not all members of any given minority group think alike. If, miraculously, something more were needed to make this point to students, surely a sufficiently diverse *reading list* would suffice.[3]

Ultimately, the university's prodiversity position prevailed as the Supreme Court upheld the law school's admission policy in *Grutter*. However, opponents of affirmative action believe that society has sacrificed fairness, a universally accepted concept, in favor of diversity, an unproven concept. They believe it is dangerous to judge anyone by the color of the skin rather than his or her achievements. Sociology professor Richard F. Tomasson writes: "It is a subversive and dangerous practice to manipulate entrance requirements by race to achieve some allegedly desirable balance . . . because it is an assault on a merit-based ethic [which] is one of the fundamental values of modern democratic society."[4] As people continue to press for anti–affirmative action laws like those adopted by California, Florida, and Texas, they advocate for the idea that fairness is more important than diversity.

> • Is it appropriate to contrast diversity with fairness? Do some people consider diversity a type of fairness?

Preferences deepen racial divides.

Opponents of affirmative action say that racial preferences deepen the racial divides that exist in society, because in any setting in which affirmative action operates, the abilities of favored groups and nonfavored groups tend to differ greatly. Dinesh D'Souza, a vocal critic of university affirmative action policies, writes that preferences do not increase the number of minorities who attend college, but instead cause the "misplacement" of many minorities in colleges for which they are not academically prepared. He writes, "[A] student . . . qualified for admission to a community college now finds himself at the University of Wisconsin. The student whose grades and extracurriculars are good enough for Wisconsin is offered admission to Bowdoin. . . . The student [qualified for Bowdoin] is accepted through affirmative action to Yale or Princeton."[5] Every person's academic abilities differ, and D'Souza believes that people should attend universities that match their abilities, rather than universities in which their abilities might not allow them to thrive.

FROM THE BENCH

The policy aspires to "achieve that diversity which has the potential to enrich everyone's education and thus make a law school class stronger than the sum of its parts." . . . The policy does not restrict the types of diversity contributions eligible for "substantial weight" in the admissions process, but instead recognizes "many possible bases for diversity admissions." . . . The policy does, however, reaffirm the law school's longstanding commitment to "one particular type of diversity," that is, "racial and ethnic diversity with special reference to the inclusion of students from groups which have been historically discriminated against, like African Americans, Hispanics and Native Americans, who without this commitment might not be represented in our student body in meaningful numbers." . . . By enrolling a "'critical mass' of [underrepresented] minority students," the law school seeks to "ensur[e] their ability to make unique contributions to the character of the law school." . . .

The policy does not define diversity "solely in terms of racial and ethnic status." . . . Nor is the policy "insensitive to the competition among all students for admission to the law school." . . . Rather, the policy seeks to guide admissions officers in "producing classes both diverse and academically outstanding, classes made up of students who promise to continue the tradition of outstanding contribution by Michigan graduates to the legal profession."

From *Grutter* v. *Bollinger*

Richard F. Tomasson charges that the differences between the academic achievement levels among various racial and ethnic groups creates an intellectual division within the student body: "Within the selective institution [affirmative action] widens the gap between, on the one hand whites and Asians, and blacks and Hispanics, on the other." He cites the examples of the University of California, Los Angeles (UCLA), Dartmouth College, and the University of Virginia: At each of these schools, the difference in average SAT scores between "disadvantaged minorities" and nonfavored groups (whites and Asian Americans) had reached 200 points.[6] The suggestion is that many minority students are not as well prepared to do the hard work required by some of these top universities because they have been

FROM THE BENCH

Dean Allan Stillwagon, who directed the law school's Office of Admissions from 1979 to 1990, explained the difficulties he encountered in defining racial groups entitled to benefit under the school's affirmative action policy. He testified that faculty members were "breathtakingly cynical" in deciding who would qualify as a member of underrepresented minorities. An example he offered was faculty debate as to whether Cubans should be counted as Hispanics: One professor objected on the grounds that Cubans were Republicans. Many academics at other law schools who are "affirmative action's more forthright defenders readily concede that diversity is merely the current rationale of convenience for a policy that they prefer to justify on other grounds.". . .

If universities are given the latitude to administer programs that are tantamount to quotas, they will have few incentives to make the existing minority admissions schemes transparent and protective of individual review. The unhappy consequence will be to perpetuate the hostilities that proper consideration of race is designed to avoid. The perpetuation, of course, would be the worst of all outcomes. Other programs do exist which will be more effective in bringing about the harmony and mutual respect among all citizens that our constitutional tradition has always sought. They, and not the program under review here, should be the model, even if the court defaults by not demanding it.

From *Grutter* v. *Bollinger* (Kennedy, J., dissenting)

"misplaced" in an overly competitive academic environment. Because whites and Asian Americans are measured solely on their abilities, it is argued, white and Asian-American students are not misplaced and therefore attend colleges where they are prepared to succeed.

Although universities are no longer segregated by law, and even though many universities have enrolled significant numbers of minority students, the integration of campuses might not be as complete as it seems on paper. At many universities, minority students primarily socialize with each other. Also, minorities have formed more or less exclusive dorms, theme houses, fraternities and sororities, and campus groups. Many universities have African-American studies departments as well. D'Souza believes that minority groups segregate themselves from the rest of the student body as a result of the gap in achievement caused by misplacement. He writes that African-American and Hispanic student groups "provide needed camaraderie," but rather than providing "academic assistance to disadvantaged students," they encourage "minority separatism and self-segregation on campus." D'Souza's explanation is that older minority students tell younger ones that their academic struggles are the result not of "insufficient academic preparation" but "pervading bigotry on campus."[7] The implication is that African-American and Hispanic groups might do more harm than good.

- **Does Dinesh D'Souza's theory explain why many campuses have active Asian-American groups?**

──────●────────────●────────────●──────

Although the Supreme Court accepted "diversity" as a constitutionally permissible basis for affirmative action in the *Grutter* decision, opponents continue to dispute its validity. They contend that diversity has no proven benefits and that efforts to increase diversity have actually resulted in racial division.

Promoting Diversity Helps Education, Business, and Democracy

n the *Grutter* decision, which upheld the University of Michigan Law School's affirmative action plan to achieve a "critical mass" of minority students in each class, the U.S. Supreme Court gave credence to a judicial philosophy penned by Justice Lewis F. Powell, Jr., in the *Bakke* case a quarter of a century earlier: that diversity is a "compelling state interest" and, therefore, that states, state universities, and employers may pursue the goal of racial and ethnic diversity without violating the Constitution. The *Grutter* decision relied on growing evidence of specific tangible benefits credited to diversity, well beyond principles of fairness or of remedying past discrimination. Despite the invalidation of the university's undergraduate affirmative action plan in the *Gratz* decision, many proponents of affirmative action considered the University of Michigan decisions an important victory. In the years since the *Bakke* decision, many universities had based their affirmative action plans on Justice Powell's model of diversity, and the University of Michigan cases made it the law of the land.

However, the University of Michigan decisions held only that states *may* institute affirmative action plans—not that they *must* do so. Proponents of affirmative action realize that not every state is convinced of diversity's benefits, as seen in the passage of anti–affirmative action measures in Texas, Florida, California, and elsewhere. Therefore, civil rights activists continue to try to shape public opinion about diversity, arguing that a diverse student body improves everyone's learning experience, that diversity in the workplace is a sound business practice, and that diversity leads to social justice and the improved functioning of American democracy.

- **Is your state likely to follow the lead of states like Texas, California, and Florida?**

Promoting diversity improves students' learning experiences.

As the Supreme Court pondered the University of Michigan cases, many educational organizations submitted *amicus* ("friend-of-the-court") briefs in an effort to influence the Court's decision. A good number of these educational organizations supported affirmative action on the grounds that diversity in the classroom improves the educational experience of minority and non-minority students. Diversity means that students are exposed to different opinions, cultures, and life experiences. According to a study of nearly 300,000 first-year college students, students in schools with more diverse student bodies had a much broader variety of opinions on topics like "racial inequity and the treatment of criminals."[1] In schools with less racial and ethnic diversity, the range of opinions was narrower.

Besides generating a diversity of opinions on topics directly linked to race, some experts believe that diverse classrooms also promote thinking skills more generally. In addition to promoting "students' intellectual and social self-concept, college satisfaction, and chances of graduating in four years," the educational groups also argued that diversity generated creative problem-solving skills:

FROM THE BENCH

We have long recognized that, given the important purpose of public education and the expansive freedoms of speech and thought associated with the university environment, universities occupy a special niche in our constitutional tradition.... In announcing the principle of student body diversity as a compelling state interest, Justice Powell invoked our cases recognizing a constitutional dimension, grounded in the First Amendment, of educational autonomy: "The freedom of a university to make its own judgments as to education includes the selection of its student body." ... From this premise, Justice Powell reasoned that by claiming "the right to select those students who will contribute the most to the 'robust exchange of ideas,'" a university "seek[s] to achieve a goal that is of paramount importance in the fulfillment of its mission." ...

[T]he law school's admissions policy promotes "cross-racial understanding," helps to break down racial stereotypes, and "enables [students] to better understand persons of different races." ... These benefits are "important and laudable," because "classroom discussion is livelier, more spirited, and simply more enlightening and interesting" when the students have "the greatest possible variety of backgrounds." ...

These benefits are not theoretical but real, as major American businesses have made clear that the skills needed in today's increasingly global marketplace can only be developed through exposure to widely diverse people, cultures, ideas, and viewpoints.... What is more, high-ranking retired officers and civilian leaders of the United States military assert that, "[b]ased on [their] decades of experience," a "highly qualified, racially diverse officer corps ... is essential to the military's ability to fulfill its principle mission to provide national security." ... The primary sources for the nation's officer corps are the service academies and the Reserve Officers Training Corps (ROTC), the latter comprising students already admitted to participating colleges and universities. ... At present, "the military cannot achieve an officer corps that is both highly qualified and racially diverse

Research also indicates that students learn more and think more actively when educated in a racially and ethnically diverse learning environment. . . . "Students learn more and think in deeper, more complex ways in a diverse educational environment."
. . . [A] diverse learning environment, a curriculum which

unless the service academies and the ROTC used limited race-conscious recruiting and admissions policies." . . .

We have repeatedly acknowledged the overriding importance of preparing students for work and citizenship, describing education as pivotal to "sustaining our political and cultural heritage" with a fundamental role in maintaining the fabric of society. . . . For this reason, the diffusion of knowledge and opportunity through public institutions of higher education must be accessible to all individuals regardless of race or ethnicity. . . .

In order to cultivate a set of leaders with legitimacy in the eyes of the citizenry, it is necessary that the path to leadership be visibly open to talented and qualified individuals of every race and ethnicity. All members of our heterogeneous society must have confidence in the openness and integrity of the educational institutions that provide this training. . . . Access to legal education (and thus the legal profession) must be inclusive of talented and qualified individuals of every race and ethnicity, so that all members of our heterogeneous society may participate in the educational institutions that provide the training and education necessary to succeed in America.

The law school does not premise its need for critical mass on "any belief that minority students always (or even consistently) express some characteristic minority viewpoint on any issue." . . . To the contrary, diminishing the force of such stereotypes is both a crucial part of the law school's mission, and one that it cannot accomplish with only token numbers of minority students. Just as growing up in a particular region or having particular professional experiences is likely to affect an individual's views, so too is one's own unique experience of being a racial minority in a society, like our own, in which race unfortunately still matters. The law school has determined, based on its experience and expertise, that a "critical mass" of underrepresented minorities is necessary to further its compelling interest in securing the educational benefits of a diverse student body.

From *Grutter* v. *Bollinger*

addresses racial issues, and engagement with peers from diverse backgrounds will result in "a learning environment that fosters conscious, effortful, deep thinking" as opposed to automatic, preconditioned responses. [2]

> • **Will people learn more about racism if more minority students are in the classroom?**

Diversity in the classroom can also have the practical effect of better preparing students for their careers. In the *Grutter* case, the Black Law Students Associations (BLSA) from three premier law schools argued that diversity in law school classrooms helps to prepare students for the practice of law: "Law school students and graduates are called upon to address enduring American dilemmas such as disparate administration of criminal justice, unequal access to health care and educational resources, and discrimination in employment. There can be no understanding of such issues without a nuanced appreciation of the persistent, though sometimes subtle, influence of race in American life." [3]

The value of diversity is also apparent to students at top law schools. The Black Law Students Associations noted that in surveys of law students at Harvard and the University of Michigan, a majority of those surveyed thought that diversity improved the exchange of ideas and helped them learn problem-solving skills. About 90 percent of students at both schools thought that racial diversity in the student body was a positive aspect of their legal education. [4]

Promoting diversity helps businesses operate more effectively.

In the University of Michigan cases, a coalition of Fortune 500 businesses submitted an *amicus* brief arguing that having a diverse workplace helps American businesses. Noting estimates that African Americans, Native Americans, Asian Americans, and Hispanics could constitute nearly half of the United States' population by the middle of the twenty-first century, the businesses considered it vital that their workforces also be diverse, to effectively serve a very diverse market for products and services. They argued:

> Because our population is diverse, and because of the increasingly global reach of American business, the skills and training needed to succeed in business today demand exposure to widely diverse people, cultures, ideas and viewpoints. Employees at every level of an organization must be able to work effectively with people who are different from themselves. [Leading businesses] need the talent and creativity of a workforce that is as diverse as the world around it.[5]

The coalition members believed that the opportunity for universities to provide diverse learning environments was therefore essential to the success of their businesses: "The rich variety of ideas, perspectives and experiences to which both non-minority and minority students are exposed in a diverse university setting, and the cross-cultural interactions they experience, are essential to the students' ability to function in and contribute to this increasingly diverse community."[6]

Although it is understandable that businesses need a diverse workforce to interact effectively with customers and understand their needs, this "rich variety of ideas" is especially critical in certain industries. The media industry, for example, has been the object of ongoing criticism. Some civil rights leaders have accused news outlets of providing coverage that is biased against minorities, and many people feel that network television does a poor job of providing entertainment programs that appeal to minority viewers, or, worse yet, offers programs that are degrading or deal in stereotypes.

In the University of Michigan cases, a coalition of media organizations argued that diversity was crucial to their business success:

> The public interest . . . is served when [our] workforces reflect the nation's diversity. Individuals whose backgrounds and life

experiences are different from the majority add to the public debate, because they bring different perspectives to bear on important issues. In addition, precisely because minority viewpoints are not monolithic, it is important for the media to include more than a token representation of minorities. Access to this broad spectrum of viewpoints both enriches the exchange of information and breaks down stereotypical assumptions about minority perspectives.[7]

As did the Fortune 500 companies, the media companies stressed that the diversity of their workforces depended both on affirmative action in hiring and promotion and the ability to hire graduates of educational institutions with affirmative action programs:

> [We] are working to improve the diversity of [our] workforces and to support minority employees as they develop and move into management positions. Despite [these] efforts . . . minority representation in the media falls far short of the goal of reflecting the diversity of the communities [we] serve. . . . [We] need talented minority and non-minority graduates who have been educated in an environment like that of University of Michigan, where differences in racial and ethnic background are valued because they add to the richness of the educational experience and to the students' preparation to contribute to the national and international exchange of ideas.[8]

* **Do businesses have a financial incentive to use affirmative action programs?**

Promoting diversity improves the functioning of a democratic society.

Several of the groups that became involved with the University of Michigan litigation were concerned about the broader

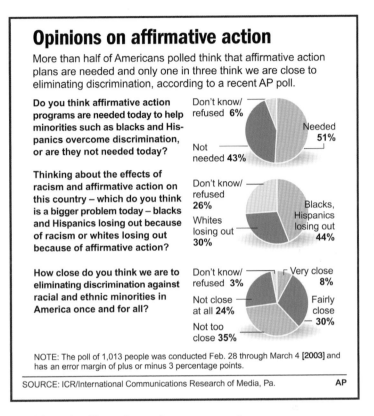

Opinions on affirmative action

More than half of Americans polled think that affirmative action plans are needed and only one in three think we are close to eliminating discrimination, according to a recent AP poll.

Do you think affirmative action programs are needed today to help minorities such as blacks and Hispanics overcome discrimination, or are they not needed today?

Don't know/ refused **6%**

Needed **51%**

Not needed **43%**

Thinking about the effects of racism and affirmative action on this country – which do you think is a bigger problem today – blacks and Hispanics losing out because of racism or whites losing out because of affirmative action?

Don't know/ refused **26%**

Whites losing out **30%**

Blacks, Hispanics losing out **44%**

How close do you think we are to eliminating discrimination against racial and ethnic minorities in America once and for all?

Don't know/ refused **3%**

Not close at all **24%**

Not too close **35%**

Very close **8%**

Fairly close **30%**

NOTE: The poll of 1,013 people was conducted Feb. 28 through March 4 [2003] and has an error margin of plus or minus 3 percentage points.

SOURCE: ICR/International Communications Research of Media, Pa.   AP

Although affirmative action programs have grown more and more unpopular over the years since the civil rights movement helped put them into effect, many Americans still believe they are needed to help level the playing field in business, education, and other opportunities. These pie charts show the responses of U.S. citizens to questions about the need for affirmative action and how it affects the American people.

societal importance of affirmative action. To some, affirmative action is necessary because when minorities achieve professional stature—that is, become doctors, lawyers, teachers, etc.—they are more likely to serve disadvantaged minority communities. This is considered vital because there are great disparities in many services; minorities have much more limited access to health care, legal representation, and business and educational opportunities.

By ending affirmative action, the argument goes, fewer minorities would achieve professional stature, and therefore, fewer people would serve minority communities, making the disparities in health care, education, and other opportunities even greater. But under current affirmative action plans, the Hispanic National Bar Association has noted that minority lawyers are more likely to serve minority communities: "There is overwhelming evidence of the need for improved legal services for people of color. . . . Minority attorneys, like doctors, have a higher rate of serving communities of color than white attorneys. Hispanic graduates are 1.4 times more likely to enter government work and 2.2 times as likely to practice public interest law. . . . "[9]

Furthermore, the lawyers' group notes, minority attorneys might have a better "connection" with their clients and can lead to hope for minority communities that often see the justice system as unfair:

> Attorneys of color will often possess an enhanced understanding of the culture and, in some cases, the language spoken in [minority] communities. . . . Hispanic communities remain underserved by the legal system, due to the paucity of attorneys who are willing and able to provide representation. Individuals facing a language barrier are often unable adequately to participate in their own representation. . . . Attorneys of color also serve as needed role models for the youth of their communities. Moreover, increased numbers of lawyers of color within the community reduced the perception of racial and ethnic bias. If admission to law schools for qualified minorities continues, the pool of lawyers of color will grow. This development will ameliorate racial and ethnic bias in our system of justice.[10]

• **Are minority doctors and lawyers needed to serve minority communities?**

In its brief in the *Grutter* case, the American Bar Association (ABA) expressed regret for its own past exclusion of minorities and argued that affirmative action is necessary to ensure that a sufficient number of minority lawyers receive training. In addition to concurring with the Hispanic National Bar Association that certain minority clients might feel more comfortable with minority lawyers, the ABA noted that access to legal training has important political ramifications in our system of government. The nation's largest lawyers' group argued: "Full participation in the legal profession by racial and ethnic minorities is [essential] for the legitimacy of our system of government. Twenty-four of our nation's forty-two presidents have been lawyers. Twenty-three of our nation's current governors hold law degrees. Lawyers have long been the single largest occupational group in the Congress. In the last session of Congress, 53 senators and 162 representatives were lawyers."[11]

When President Bill Clinton was elected in 1992, he promised that his cabinet would "look like America"—meaning that he was dedicated to appointing women and minorities to important positions. However, at present, court systems, police departments, and government bureaucracies often do not reflect the racial diversity of the people whom they serve. Without affirmative action programs, many believe, progress toward a more representative government will be halted.

The *Grutter* decision was a landmark ruling because it embraced the concept of diversity. Proponents of affirmative action believe that diversity is beneficial to education, business, and the functioning of our democracy.

Preferences Are Harmful to Recipients and "Nonfavored" Minorities

M any opponents of affirmative action policies are white males, and many opponents also think of the primary "victims" of "reverse discrimination" as being white males. However, not all opponents of affirmative action are white males, and many opponents believe that affirmative action victimizes people other than white males—including the people such policies are intended to help.

Sometimes, people doubt the abilities of all minorities, thinking that any success they have can be attributed to affirmative action. Journalist Ruben Navarrette, Jr., who is Mexican-American, recalls what happened when he was admitted to Harvard. Despite "four years of hard work [in high school] and perfect grades," he writes, "white classmates, many with grades not as good as mine and reeling from rejections by the schools that were admitting me, were far more direct. 'Now, you know, if you hadn't been Mexican . . . ,' one said."[1] Though his essay supports affirmative action, it points out one major criticism of racial preferences: that affirmative action makes people discount the abilities of minorities.

Hillary Chen had a very different experience when it came to affirmative action. In 1993, her family moved from one San Francisco neighborhood to another, and the school system told Hillary's parents that she could not attend any of the three elementary schools nearest to the family's new house. At the time, the San Francisco school system had an affirmative action plan that guaranteed various minority groups places at each school. But the only way to reserve spots for members of some minority groups was to limit the number of spots for white children and other minority groups. Chinese-American students were "capped out" at the local schools—meaning that the schools had room for members of other racial and ethnic groups but could not admit any more Chinese Americans. Her family brought a lawsuit in federal court[2] that ultimately forced the school system to rethink its quotas. Critics of racial preferences say that schools, employers, and governments cannot help some deserving people without inadvertently hurting others.

> • **If quotas on "disadvantaged" minorities are illegal, should caps on other minorities or whites be legal?**

Minorities suffer from stigma even if they do not benefit from affirmative action.

Ruben Navarrette, Jr.'s story—that his classmates had dismissed his achievements and credited affirmative action for his admission to Harvard—is unfortunately all too typical, opponents of racial preferences say. They say that affirmative action policies attach a stigma—or undesirable mark—to all minorities whether they have actually benefited from affirmative action or not. Because these policies help some people who are unqualified—in some people's opinion—for schools, jobs, and government contracts, people will assume that any members of a minority group who have achieved any type of success have done so only because of preferential treatment. This stigma can be internal as well: People who have benefited from affirmative action programs can lose confidence in their abilities and think they have achieved their success only because of such programs.

In opposition to the University of Michigan's use of race as a factor in admissions, the Pacific Legal Foundation, a conservative

FROM THE BENCH

These different numbers, moreover, come only as a result of substantially different treatment among the three underrepresented minority groups, as is apparent in an example offered by the law school and highlighted by the court: The school asserts that it "frequently accepts nonminority applicants with grades and test scores lower than underrepresented minority applicants (and other non-minority applicants) who are rejected." . . . Specifically, the law school states that "[s]ixty-nine minority applicants were rejected between 1995 and 2000 with at least a 3.5 [grade point average (GPA)] and a [score of] 159 or higher on the [Law School Admission Test (LSAT)]" while a number of Caucasian and Asian American applicants with similar or lower scores were admitted. . . .

Review of the record reveals only 67 such individuals. Of these 67 individuals, 56 were Hispanic, while only 6 were African American, and only 5 were Native American. This discrepancy reflects a consistent practice. For example, in 2000, 12 Hispanics who scored between a 159–160 on the LSAT and earned a GPA of 3.00 or higher applied for admission and only 2 were admitted. . . . Meanwhile, 12 African Americans in the same range of qualifications applied for admission and all 12 were admitted. . . . Likewise, that same year, 16 Hispanics who scored between a 151–153 on the LSAT and earned a 3.00 or higher applied for admission and only 1 of those applicants was admitted. . . . Twenty-three similarly qualified African Americans applied for admission and 14 were admitted. . . .

These statistics have a significant bearing on petitioner's case. Respondents have never offered any race-specific arguments explaining why significantly more individuals from one underrepresented minority group are needed in order to achieve "critical mass" or further student body diversity. They certainly public interest law firm, argued: "A plausible and harmful effect of the University of Michigan's race-based policy is that it brands the admitted minority students as underachievers who need assistance in the form of preferences to gain entry to the university. . . . Such a damaging stereotype can undermine the self-esteem of minority students and create questions as to their achievements and qualifications."[3]

Another conservative group, the Claremont Institute,

have not explained why Hispanics, who they have said are among "the groups most isolated by racial barriers in our country," should have their admission capped out in this manner. . . . True, petitioner is neither Hispanic nor Native American. But the law school's disparate admissions practices with respect to these minority groups demonstrate that its alleged goal of "critical mass" is simply a sham. Petitioner may use these statistics to expose this sham, which is the basis for the law school's admission of less qualified underrepresented minorities in preference to her. Surely strict scrutiny cannot permit these sort of disparities without at least some explanation.

Only when the "critical mass" label is discarded does a likely explanation for these numbers emerge. The court states that the law school's goal of attaining a "critical mass" of underrepresented minority students is not an interest in merely "'assur[ing] within its student body some specified percentage of a particular group merely because of its race or ethnic origin.'" . . . The court recognizes that such an interest "would amount to outright racial balancing, which is patently unconstitutional." . . .

But the correlation between the percentage of the law school's pool of applicants who are members of the three minority groups and the percentage of the admitted applicants who are members of these same groups is far too precise to be dismissed as merely the result of the school paying "some attention to [the] numbers." [F]rom 1995 through 2000 the percentage of admitted applicants who were members of these minority groups closely tracked the percentage of individuals in the school's applicant pool who were from the same groups.

From *Grutter* v. *Bollinger* (Rehnquist, C.J., dissenting)

labeled affirmative action programs as paternalistic attempts to help minorities that wind up doing more harm than good. The group, of which former U.S. Attorney General Ed Meese is a member, likened affirmative action programs to "legislation that once blocked women from entering a variety of professions which was 'apparently designed to benefit or protect women. . . .'" The group argued in the University of Michigan cases: "In exactly the same way, racial preferences, whether in hiring or contracting, the provision of government benefits, or, as here, in law school and college admissions, are ostensibly designed to shield minority group members, but in fact are premised on the notion that they are incapable of competing without a big brother—a white big brother—to guide them."[4]

Perhaps the biggest problem with the stigma created by affirmative action is that there is no way for the truly qualified minority candidates—the ones who would have been admitted or hired without the benefit of affirmative action—to distinguish themselves from those whose test scores or job qualifications alone were not enough. In *Ending Affirmative Action*, Terry Eastland writes: "The generalization is that 'minority' equals 'affirmative action' equals 'lower standards.' . . . Tragically, this process of generalization and inference trails the many minorities—perhaps the majority—who make their way without the 'help' of any preferential treatment."[5]

Larry Elder, a conservative talk-show host who is African-American, firmly believes that affirmative action leads to self-stigmatization, meaning that people who benefit from affirmative action lose faith in their own abilities and attribute their success solely to affirmative action. In his book, he recalls meeting an African-American man who challenged Elder's public opposition to affirmative action; the man told Elder that he had become a successful lawyer only because Loyola University had an affirmative action program. Elder bristled at this suggestion, telling the man that even without affirmative action, he certainly could have attended law school elsewhere. Elder

FROM THE BENCH

The law school is not looking for those students who, despite a lower LSAT score or undergraduate grade point average, will succeed in the study of law. The law school seeks only a facade—it is sufficient that the class looks right, even if it does not perform right.

The law school tantalizes unprepared students with the promise of a University of Michigan degree and all of the opportunities that it offers. These overmatched students take the bait, only to find that they cannot succeed in the cauldron of competition.... Indeed, to cover the tracks of the aestheticists, this cruel farce of racial discrimination must continue—in selection for the Michigan Law Review, ...and in hiring at law firms and for judicial clerkships—until the "beneficiaries" are no longer tolerated. While these students may graduate with law degrees, there is no evidence that they have received a qualitatively better legal education (or become better lawyers) than if they had gone to a less "elite" law school for which they were better prepared. And the aestheticists will never address the real problems facing "underrepresented minorities," instead continuing their social experiments on other people's children.

Beyond the harm the law school's racial discrimination visits upon its test subjects, no social science has disproved the notion that this discrimination "engender[s] attitudes of superiority or, alternatively, provoke[s] resentment among those who believe that they have been wronged by the government's use of race." [Affirmative action] programs stamp minorities with a badge of inferiority and may cause them to develop dependencies or to adopt an attitude that they are 'entitled' to preferences....

It is uncontested that each year, the law school admits a handful of blacks who would be admitted in the absence of racial discrimination.... Who can differentiate between those who belong and those who do not? The majority of blacks are admitted to the law school because of discrimination, and because of this policy all are tarred as undeserving. This problem of stigma does not depend on determinacy as to whether those stigmatized are actually the "beneficiaries" of racial discrimination. When blacks take positions in the highest places of government, industry, or academia, it is an open question today whether their skin color played a part in their advancement. The question itself is the stigma—because either racial discrimination did play a role, in which case the person may be deemed "otherwise unqualified," or it did not, in which case asking the question itself unfairly marks those blacks who would succeed without discrimination.

From *Grutter* v. *Bollinger* (Thomas, J., concurring in part and dissenting in part)

writes, "This 'but-for-affirmative-action-I'd-be-driving-a-truck' mentality is yet another unintended consequence of preferences. . . . Without drive, study, and sense of purpose, all the preferential programs in the world wouldn't have helped this guy."[6]

> • **Do arguments about stigma have validity when minorities make the arguments? What about when white people make the arguments?**

Affirmative action programs ignore the underlying problems faced by minorities.

Some opponents believe that affirmative action harms not only individual recipients but also helps to keep "disadvantaged" minority groups disadvantaged. Members of minority groups in the United States—particularly African Americans and Hispanics—disproportionately make up the most disadvantaged economic class in America. With untold tens of thousands of minorities living in poverty, some opponents of affirmative action say, plans to admit a handful of minority students into elite universities is equivalent to putting a band-aid on a gaping wound.

In his criticism of affirmative action, sociology professor Richard Tomasson writes that such programs have benefited only a small number of minorities, while most are left to live in poverty:

> What has happened to the black population [since the advent of affirmative action] has been a huge and healthy increase in its proportions . . . in white-collar occupations, and in the skilled trades. At the same time the plight of inner-city blacks has horribly worsened, reaching epic levels of illegitimacy, teen pregnancy, crime, mental retardation, obesity, drug addiction, AIDS, welfare dependence, and paranoid victim-ization. . . . Affirmative action has helped the former group to some unknowable extent, but has been irrelevant to the latter.

Tomasson dismisses the argument that affirmative action is needed to help the disproportionate number of minorities living in poverty, saying that affirmative action has failed to address the issues. Despite decades of affirmative action, he writes, "no other rich democracy in the world has spawned an underclass of such dimensions as the United States. And numerically, most are black."[7]

In the University of Michigan cases, many African-American groups supported the university's use of racial preferences; however, one group of African-American leaders argued that affirmative action at the university level is no solution to the vast problems facing minorities today. The Center for New Black Leadership wrote:

> [The] massive racial preferences employed by [the university] are a superficial and self-defeating response to a serious national problem . . . a chronic and debilitating academic gap, which manifests itself in severe racial disparities in admissions at elite institutions of higher learning. Racial preferences do nothing to close that academic gap. . . . To close the academic gap requires efforts far more systematic than those employed by . . . most government entities.[8]

• Is a partial solution better than no solution?

The problem, the group argued, is that educational disparities are simply too widespread to be addressed with individual affirmative action policies; instead, broad efforts are needed to ensure that every child has an opportunity for a quality education, beginning in his or her youth. The group praised, for example, efforts by the University of California (which is prohibited by law from using racial preferences) to help disadvantaged students prepare for—and qualify for—a college education by encouraging professors and college students to tutor and mentor students from disadvantaged backgrounds.

Even people who seemingly benefit from admission or job preferences might end up suffering harm in the long run, writes social scientist Charles Murray. In his essay, "Affirmative Racism," Murray gives the example of an African-American man who is accepted to college and then business school under affirmative action programs. After business school, despite average grades, he lands a job with a company eager to increase the "diversity" of its workforce. After he is hired, rather than receiving "scut work" like his white colleagues, he is taken to meetings so the company can impress its clients with its "diverse" workforce. Although the man's supervisors might think they are doing him a favor by sparing him the unpleasant tasks, they are inadvertently denying him the opportunity to learn on the job so he has the skills needed for advancement. Murray writes: "There are a variety of requirements to be met

FROM THE BENCH

Indeed, the very existence of racial discrimination of the type practiced by the law school may impede the narrowing of the LSAT testing gap. An applicant's LSAT score can improve dramatically with preparation, but such preparation is a cost, and there must be sufficient benefits attached to an improved score to justify additional study. Whites scoring between 163 and 167 on the LSAT are routinely rejected by the law school, and thus whites aspiring to admission at the law school have every incentive to improve their score to levels above that range. Blacks, on the other hand, are nearly guaranteed admission if they score above 155.... As admission prospects approach certainty, there is no incentive for the black applicant to continue to prepare for the LSAT once he is reasonably assured of achieving the requisite score. It is far from certain that the LSAT test-taker's behavior is responsive to the law school's admissions policies. Nevertheless, the possibility remains that this racial discrimination will help fulfill the bigot's prophecy about black underperformance—just as it confirms the conspiracy theorist's belief that "institutional racism" is at fault for every racial disparity in our society.

From *Grutter* v. *Bollinger* (Thomas, J., concurring in part and dissenting in part)

and rituals to be observed for which a black face is helpful. These have little to do with the long-term career interests of the new employee; on the contrary, they often lead to a dead-end job as head of the minority-relations section of the personnel department." Eventually, Murray believes, a person must define his or her own career, and to the extent that affirmative action denies people the opportunity to "learn things the hard way," it can undermine the career prospects of beneficiaries.[9]

Preferring select minority groups harms other minority groups.

Proponents of affirmative action programs usually describe them in terms of "helping" people, yet critics believe the programs harm others. In general, an affirmative action program favors certain minorities for scarce resources: There are only a limited number of spots at a university, a limited number of jobs, and a limited number of government contracts. Therefore, for each person who is helped by affirmative action to get that college acceptance, job, or contract, another person is harmed by *not* having the chance to get that benefit. There is a misperception, opponents of racial preferences say, that the people denied these benefits are all white males, who because of societal racism and prosperity do not need these benefits anyway. Although most opponents of affirmative action would argue that it is not fair to discriminate against white males, they also believe that affirmative action programs discriminate against minority groups that do not benefit from the programs.

Most affirmative action programs—including those used by the University of Michigan—do not favor all minority groups but only those considered "disadvantaged" or "underrepresented." The University of Michigan, for example, gives special consideration to African Americans, Hispanics, and Native Americans. It does not, however, give special preferences to members of other racial minority groups, like Asian Americans, or religious or ethnic minorities, such as Jews and Polish Americans.

Conservative jurist Robert Bork criticizes giving preferences to groups that are "underrepresented." He recalls a White House meeting during which a man suggested that people of Slavic ancestry receive preference in admissions because some Slavic groups had fewer people, percentage-wise, attending college than African Americans, who are included in university affirmative action programs. The man's suggestion that a European ethnic group receive preferential treatment was dismissed as ridiculous by those present, but Bork believes that the comment shows that preferences, once started, have no ending point. He writes:

> If lack of proportional representation is inequitable, it becomes impossible to see why all groups whose proportion in employment, college, or what have you falls below its proportion of the population should not benefit from the principle.... [W]e tend to talk of "blacks" or "whites," but in fact there is great ethnic diversity within each of these groups and even within such subgroups as Slavs or Catholics or Jews. [10]

- **Is there a way to help disadvantaged minorities without hurting other people?**

The dark side of combating "underrepresentation" is that it is often coupled with a process that critics call "capping out." Just as certain minority groups are "underrepresented"—meaning that the percentage of Hispanics at a university is smaller than the percentage of Hispanics in the state or the country—there are also groups that must be considered "overrepresented." Often, universities have a larger percentage of Asian Americans or Jews in their student bodies than are present in society. But can a minority group be "overrepresented"? Critics of affirmative action think not. Dinesh D'Souza has criticized prestigious universities—though they "strenuously deny" it—of limiting the number of Asian students. He writes: "For Asian Americans, the cruel irony is that preferential admissions policies, which are set up to atone for discrimination, seem to have institutionalized and legitimized discrimination against a minority group that is itself the victim of continuing prejudice in America."[11]

The so-called problem is that Asian Americans, as a subgroup of the population, tend to have proportionately higher test scores and grades than other subgroups. Therefore, in a completely

FROM THE BENCH

The court's observation that race-conscious programs "must have a logical end point" . . . accords with the international understanding of the office of affirmative action. The International Convention on the Elimination of All Forms of Racial Discrimination, ratified by the United States in 1994 . . . endorses "special and concrete measures to ensure the adequate development and protection of certain racial groups or individuals belonging to them, for the purpose of guaranteeing them the full and equal enjoyment of human rights and fundamental freedoms." . . . But such measures, the convention instructs, "shall in no case entail as a consequence the maintenance of unequal or separate rights for different racial groups after the objectives for which they were taken have been achieved." . . .

It is well documented that conscious and unconscious race bias, even rank discrimination based on race, remain alive in our land, impeding realization of our highest values and ideals. . . . And schools in predominantly minority communities lag far behind others measured by the educational resources available to them. . . .

However strong the public's desire for improved education systems may be . . . it remains the current reality that many minority students encounter markedly inadequate and unequal educational opportunities. Despite these inequalities, some minority students are able to meet the high threshold requirements set for admission to the country's finest undergraduate and graduate educational institutions. As lower school education in minority communities improves, an increase in the number of such students may be anticipated. From today's vantage point, one may hope, but not firmly forecast, that over the next generation's span, progress toward nondiscrimination and genuinely equal opportunity will make it safe to sunset affirmative action.

Source: *Grutter v. Bollinger* (Ginsburg, J., concurring)

merit-based, color-blind admissions program, Asian Americans, despite being a small minority of the population, would make up a much larger percentage of university enrollment. Therefore, supposedly in the name of diversity, universities—and even the school system in San Francisco—have "capped out" Asian Americans who deserved to attend the schools. As the Asian American Legal Foundation points out:

> A notorious manifestation of this racial ceiling was at Lowell High School, considered the best high school in the district and one of the best in California. . . . Because admission on a strictly by-the-numbers basis would have caused Lowell's student body to be more than 40 percent Chinese American, the San Francisco school district required Chinese American applicants to score higher than members of any other racial group, including white, Korean, and Japanese, to gain admission.[12]

• **How narrowly should a group be defined when it comes to determining "underrepresentation"? Are there not also many groups within the larger group of Hispanics?**

Asian Americans have not been the only victims of affirmative action; some charge that "diversity" programs at elite universities began as efforts to exclude Jewish students, who early in the twentieth century began to make up a statistically disproportionate percentage of university student bodies. Dissenting in the *Grutter* case, Justice Clarence Thomas wrote:

> [S]elective admissions [originated] in the beginning of the twentieth century, as universities sought to exercise more control over the composition of their student bodies. Since its inception, selective admissions has been the vehicle for racial, ethnic, and religious tinkering and experimentation by university administrators. The initial driving force . . . was the same desire to select racial winners and losers. . . . Columbia,

Harvard, and others infamously determined that they had "too many" Jews. . . . Columbia employed intelligence tests precisely because Jewish applicants, who were predominantly immigrants, scored worse on such tests. . . . [T]he tests were adopted with full knowledge of their disparate impact.[13]

Many opponents of affirmative action strongly believe that for every "winner," there is a "loser," and, therefore, racial preferences are just as bad as any other type of discrimination.

———————•———————•———————•———————

Critics of affirmative action believe that such policies fail in their stated goal of helping members of minority groups. Not only do the programs cause problems for recipients—like a perception that minorities cannot succeed on their own merits—but they ignore the real problems faced by the poorest Americans and even discriminate against some minority groups that have been the victims of past negative bias.

Affirmative Action Policies Help People for Whom the Playing Field Is Not Level

Tanya Barrientos of the *Philadelphia Inquirer* tells the story of Macarena Hernandez as an example of how affirmative action helps people rise out of poverty. Born to Mexican immigrant parents, in childhood, Hernandez became a migrant farmworker, picking grapes and doing other jobs. Despite her responsibilities, she was an excellent student, and although her parents did not think college was worthwhile, she talked them into letting her go. She was a talented young journalist who served internships at the *Inquirer* and *The New York Times* before eventually becoming a reporter for a newspaper in San Antonio, Texas. Affirmative action programs helped her attend quality universities and gain experience in internships designed for minority journalists, and she successfully made the transition from migrant laborer to accomplished journalist. Barrientos calls her "an

74

example of the sort of talent that a top-notch affirmative-action program can discover."[1]

Stories like these are by no means unusual. Supporters of affirmative action dismiss opponents' claims that the programs are harmful to minorities, saying that any stigma created by affirmative action is no worse than the discrimination that already exists in society. Furthermore, they say, affirmative action programs benefit minority groups in general rather than a select few people and focus on helping those minority groups that need help the most. Although affirmative action might not solve all of society's problems, its supporters say that it must be maintained while society continues to address problems facing minority groups, like poverty, failing schools, and poor health.

THE LETTER OF THE LAW

A student applying for admission who does not meet [GPA and standardized testing] requirements may be eligible for admission through a student profile assessment which considers additional factors, including but not limited to, the following: family educational background, socioeconomic status, graduate of a low-performing high school, international baccalaureate program graduate, geographic location, and special talents. These additional factors shall not include preferences in the admissions process for applicants on the basis of race, national origin, or sex.... [This] system is limited each year to 10 percent of the total system first-time-in-college students....

A student applying for admission who is a graduate of a public Florida high school, has completed nineteen (19) required high school units . . . ranks in the top 20 percent of his/her high school graduating class, and who has submitted test scores from the [SAT or ACT] shall be admitted to a university in the State University System....

Neither State University System nor individual university admissions criteria shall include preferences in the admissions process for applicants on the basis of race, national origin, or sex.

Source: Florida Administrative Code Sec. 6C-6.002 (2002)

The problem of stigma is exaggerated.

Some social scientists discount the notion that affirmative action causes internal stigma—minorities doubting their own abilities. In "Ten Myths About Affirmative Action," Scott Plous cites data from a 1995 Gallup Poll of African Americans and white women in the workforce. He writes that nearly 90 percent of those surveyed had not felt that "others questioned their abilities because of affirmative action. . . . [This reaction] is understandable—after all, white men, who have traditionally benefited from preferential hiring, do not feel hampered by self-doubt or a loss in self-esteem. . . . [In] many cases, affirmative action may actually raise the self-esteem of women and minorities by providing them with employment and opportunities for advancement."[2] In other words, minorities and women actually might feel more motivated and self-confident if they know that affirmative action programs will help them avoid being denied advancement due to discrimination.

Additionally, the problem of internal stigma, some believe, is overshadowed by the frustration felt by minorities (and women) at being denied opportunities, with or without affirmative action policies in place. It is important to remember that many qualified women and minorities have not achieved the same status as white men, who continue to hold most executive jobs, college professorships, elected offices, and other positions of prestige. Psychology professors Faye J. Crosby and Sharon D. Herzberger explain: "When women and people of color perceive themselves to be deprived relative to equally talented members of other groups, they . . . can become frustrated, resentful, and even downright hostile."[3] Many people say that the business world has a "glass ceiling" for women and minorities. What this means is that women and minorities may advance to a certain point, and although they can see the next level, they cannot get there because of discrimination. For many, the glass ceiling means they reach the highest level of "middle management" but are shut out of top positions, like chief executive officer and corporate vice president. Reaching the glass ceiling can be particularly frustrating because rising to that level requires talent and hard work, but factors beyond a person's control keep him or her from the top jobs.

Furthermore, many people reject claims that affirmative action causes external stigma—other people doubting minorities' abilities. Crosby and Herzberger write, "[L]et's be realistic. People of color and women suffered from suspicions about their competence long before affirmative action programs gave people an excuse for being suspicious."[4]

• **Why is there a "glass ceiling" for women and minorities?**

Many other preferences help people in society, yet nobody criticizes these as stigmatizing. For example, white business owners might be likely to hire their white relatives. Additionally, children of university alumni are given a "legacy" preference when applying to college, allowing the student to carry on his or her parent's legacy at the school. Many believe that this type of preference disproportionately favors white applicants because universities might have excluded the parents of African-American applicants. Kim Gandy, the president of the National Organization for Women (NOW), criticized President George W. Bush for opposing race-based affirmative action policies. She writes, "There is little doubt that George W. Bush's grades were lower than those of hundreds of students who were rejected by Yale University the same year Bush was welcomed there. . . . [He] was a beneficiary of one kind of affirmative action—the kind that favored the sons of overwhelmingly white and well-to-do Yale graduates."[5] In her opinion, it was hypocritical for the Bush White House to oppose affirmative action while not challenging policies that allowed universities to favor white applicants.

• **Is it fair to compare "legacy admissions" to affirmative action programs?**

Some people compare affirmative action programs with university "legacy" policies under which students may be admitted because of a parent's previous attendance at the college. This political cartoon pokes fun at this kind of preferential treatment in which someone who is otherwise unqualified for admission might get into college because of a parent's legacy.

Affirmative action helps all members of disadvantaged minority groups.

Answering a common criticism of affirmative action—that it helps only a privileged few members of minority groups, while leaving many others living in poverty—some supporters of affirmative action believe that a partial solution is better than no solution at all. For example, a major problem facing minorities is substandard elementary and secondary education, primarily caused by a lack of funding in minority-dominated school districts. In the *Gratz* case, involving the University of Michigan's undergraduate admission policies, a group of sixty members of the U.S. Congress argued that while the long-term goal should be to fix inequalities in school funding, affirmative action is a necessary solution until equality in funding is achieved. The representatives wrote:

> [R]emedial efforts can take years to implement—in some cases nearly 30 years—and generations of students of color fail to advance in life because their beginnings were stunted by a lack of opportunity in education. . . . Overwhelmingly, the students who are most significantly disadvantaged are of racial and ethnic minority backgrounds. . . . [College] administrators [should] do what they can to right these imbalances by taking students' race into account in the admissions process.[6]

Others dispute the notion that affirmative action really is a partial solution. Groups like the NAACP and ACLU think that such criticisms ignore the immense impact that racism has taken on America's minorities, and, therefore, ignore the immense benefit that such programs can provide. In the University of Michigan cases, the groups argued:

In the absence of slavery, *de jure* segregation, and persistent "societal discrimination," this generation of applicants might have lived in a society where 700,000 more African Americans have jobs, and nearly two million more African Americans hold higher paying and managerial jobs. They might have lived in a society where the average African American household earns 56 percent more than at present, and altogether, African American households earn another $190 billion. . . .

African Americans could have owned over 600,000 more businesses, with $2.7 trillion more in revenues. . . . Two million more African Americans could have high school diplomas, and nearly two million more could have undergraduate degrees.[7]

In effect, helping some minorities really can help the entire minority community through a "trickle-down" effect. In much the same way that minority doctors and lawyers are more likely to serve minority clients and patients, it can be argued that minority-owned businesses create jobs for minorities, that higher wages for minorities help them improve their homes and their neighborhoods, and that affirmative action has other indirect effects.

> • **Is it realistic to think that affirmative action programs could be expanded in today's political environment?**

There are valid reasons for helping select minority groups.

One of Scott Plous's "Ten Myths About Affirmative Action" is, "If Jewish people and Asian Americans can rapidly advance economically, African Americans should be able to do the same." According to Plous, the important difference to consider is that African Americans have been subjected to slavery and other forms of institutional racism, while "Jews and Asians, on the other hand, immigrated to North America—often as doctors, lawyers, professors, and entrepreneurs and so forth. Moreover, European Jews were able to function as part of the white majority."[8] Similar arguments could be made that Italian Americans, Irish Americans, and other ethnic groups who have suffered from previous societal discrimination have effectively "integrated" themselves into the white majority.

Supreme Court Justice Ruth Bader Ginsburg agrees that there is ample justification for helping certain minority groups through affirmative action programs while not helping other minority groups. Dissenting from the Court's invalidation of

FROM THE BENCH

The court also holds that racial discrimination in admissions should be given another 25 years before it is deemed no longer narrowly tailored to the law school's fabricated compelling state interest.... While I agree that in 25 years the practices of the law school will be illegal, they are . . . illegal now. The majority does not and cannot rest its time limitation on any evidence that the gap in credentials between black and white students is shrinking or will be gone in that timeframe. In recent years there has been virtually no change, for example, in the proportion of law school applicants with LSAT scores of 165 and higher who are black. In 1993 blacks constituted 1.1 percent of law school applicants in that score range, though they represented 11.1 percent of all applicants.... No one can seriously contend, and the court does not, that the racial gap in academic credentials will disappear in 25 years. Nor is the court's holding that racial discrimination will be unconstitutional in 25 years made contingent on the gap closing in that time.

Source: *Grutter* v. *Bollinger* (Thomas, J., concurring in part and dissenting in part)

the University of Michigan's undergraduate admission policy in *Gratz*, Justice Ginsburg wrote:

> The racial and ethnic groups to which the college accords special consideration [African Americans, Hispanics, and Native Americans] historically have been relegated to inferior status by law and social practice; their members continue to experience class-based discrimination to this day.... There is no suggestion that the college adopted its current policy in order to limit or decrease enrollment by any particular racial or ethnic group, and no seats are reserved on the basis of race.... Nor has there been any demonstration that the college's program unduly constricts admissions opportunities for students who do not receive special consideration based on race.[9]

- **Do you agree with Justice Ginsburg's belief that affirmative action programs do not harm "nonfavored" groups?**

FROM THE BENCH

Our jurisprudence ranks race a "suspect" category, "not because [race] is inevitably an impermissible classification, but because it is one which usually, to our national shame, has been drawn for the purpose of maintaining racial inequality."... But where race is considered "for the purpose of achieving equality,"... no automatic proscription is in order. For, as insightfully explained, "[t]he Constitution is both color-blind and color conscious. To avoid conflict with the equal protection clause, a classification that denies a benefit, causes harm, or imposes a burden must not be based on race. In that sense, the Constitution is color-blind. But the Constitution is color conscious to prevent discrimination being perpetuated and to undo the effects of past discrimination."

From *Gratz* v. *Bollinger* (Ginsburg, J., dissenting)

Supporters of affirmative action deny that preferences stigmatize minorities; instead, they believe that affirmative action helps a wide range of people succeed. Supporters also believe that there is ample justification for helping groups, like African Americans, Hispanics, and Native Americans, who suffer disproportionate levels of poverty and low-quality education.

Conclusion:
The Future of
Affirmative Action

The effects of the Supreme Court's decisions in the University of Michigan cases remain to be seen. With both sides hailing victory, picking a winner might be very difficult. However, affirmative action supporters definitely won at least a partial victory, to the extent that the politically conservative court did not strike down racial preferences across the board, something many observers had predicted the justices might do. Most likely, the practical result will be that most current affirmative action programs will be unaffected by the decision, which essentially adopted the "diversity" theory first suggested by Justice Lewis F. Powell, Jr., twenty-five years earlier, and upon which many schools (and employers) had based their affirmative action programs. In short, universities may use affirmative action programs if needed to increase the representation of minorities in their student bodies. By implication, employers may use affirmative action to increase minority representation in the workforce.

Future cases might involve challenges to other affirmative action policies, on the grounds that they do not give individualized attention to each college applicant or job candidate. This individualized attention was central to the University of Michigan cases, in which the Supreme Court struck down the undergraduate college's policy of awarding twenty points (on a scale of 150) to each minority applicant, but upheld the law school's policy of considering race as a factor in admission in a less concrete manner. It can be expected that conservative law firms will help bring lawsuits on behalf of whites and Asian Americans who feel they have been the victims of "reverse discrimination."

> • **Will the court system face a barrage of lawsuits challenging whether affirmative action programs are individualized?**

Opponents of affirmative action will continue to wage the battle against preferences, both in the "court of public opinion," and at the state level. Three of the most populous states—California, Texas, and Florida—have eliminated affirmative action policies. They are also three of the states with the largest minority populations, so these policies have begun to have a profound effect. The most noticeable effect has been to replace affirmative action in college admissions with a system under which people who graduate at the top of their class are guaranteed admission to state universities. This way, top students at predominantly African-American or Hispanic schools are able to attend college without the use of outright racial preferences.

Supporters of these types of laws, frequently called "percentage plans," passed by California, Texas, and Florida, are trying to persuade voters in other states to support such resolutions, but many would like to see the laws taken even further. They are calling for a completely "color-blind" system of law, in which the government is not allowed to consider race in any type of decision. But is the nation ready for such laws?

Can Percentage Plans Replace Affirmative Action?

In the University of Michigan cases, the U.S. government filed an *amicus* brief—the nation was not a party in the lawsuit—opposing affirmative action plans and promoting race-neutral "percentage plans." In states with these plans, students who graduate in the top part of their class are guaranteed admission to the states' universities. For example, in Texas, the top 10 percent of the class is guaranteed admission to *any* of the state's public universities; in Florida, a student graduating in the top 20 percent of his or her class is guaranteed admission to *at least one* of the state's public universities. A significant number of minority students graduate near the top of their graduating class, and in schools in which minorities make up a majority of the student body, they also often make up the majority of students who qualify for automatic admission under these plans.

THE LETTER OF THE LAW

E ach general academic teaching institution shall admit an applicant for admission to the institution as an undergraduate student if the applicant graduated with a grade point average in the top 10 percent of the student's high school graduating class in one of the two school years preceding the academic year for which the applicant is applying for admission and the applicant graduated from a public or private high school in this state accredited by a generally recognized accrediting organization or from a high school operated by the United States Department of Defense. . . .

After admitting an applicant under this section, the institution shall review the applicant's record and any other factor the institution considers appropriate to determine whether the applicant may require additional preparation for college-level work or would benefit from inclusion in a retention program. The institution may require a student so identified to enroll during the summer immediately after the student is admitted under this section to participate in appropriate enrichment courses and orientation programs.

From Tex. Educ. Code § 51.803.

- **Would a student who was in the top 5 percent of his or her class have a reason not to transfer to a better school?**

The federal government's support of percentage plans came as no surprise, because George W. Bush had instituted Texas's plan while he was governor of the Lone Star state, and his brother Jeb is the governor responsible for Florida's plan. In its brief, the federal government noted that Texas universities have experienced minority enrollments similar to those before affirmative action was abolished in 1996. In California and Florida, the numbers of certain minority groups at certain schools has declined, but the overall number of minority students has remained constant or increased.

Critics of percentage plans say that they have several flaws. Foremost, they rely on and perpetuate segregation because they rely on segregated schools: Most of the minority students

FROM THE BENCH

I believe blacks can achieve in every avenue of American life without the meddling of university administrators. Because I wish to see all students succeed whatever their color, I share, in some respect, the sympathies of those who sponsor the type of discrimination advanced by the University of Michigan Law School.... The Constitution does not, however, tolerate institutional devotion to the status quo in admissions policies when such devotion ripens into racial discrimination. Nor does the Constitution countenance the unprecedented deference the court gives to the law school, an approach inconsistent with the very concept of "strict scrutiny."

No one would argue that a university could set up a lower general admission standard and then impose heightened requirements only on black applicants. Similarly, a university may not maintain a high admission standard and grant exemptions to favored races. The law school, of its own choosing, and for its own purposes, maintains an exclusionary admissions system that it knows produces racially disproportionate results. Racial discrimination is not a permissible solution to the self-inflicted wounds of this elitist admissions policy.

From *Grutter* v. *Bollinger* (Thomas, J., concurring in part and dissenting in part)

who qualify do so by graduating near the top of their class in predominantly minority schools. As a number of members of Congress argued in the *Gratz* case: "[The] most shocking reality of the percentage plans . . . is that the students in Texas, California, and Florida are being educated in racially segregated schools reminiscent of a painful history this country and the courts have long fought to overcome."[1] People who advocate for percentage plans are surely aware that their "success" in placing minority students relies on schools that are heavily segregated.

Moreover, percentage plans would work only—if at all—in states with large public university systems, like those in Texas, California, and Florida. And the plans leave many situations unaddressed: The plans do not guarantee diversity in graduate school admissions. For example, a coalition of Black Law Students Associations pointed out that the enrollment of African Americans at the University of California's law schools and the University of Texas Law School has decreased since affirmative action policies were abolished in the late 1990s. Also, a group of educational organizations led by the American Educational Research Association pointed out that such policies cannot be used by smaller state schools or private institutions, which do not have the resources or the desire to admit every student who graduates within a certain percentage of his or her high school class.

Can the United States Become a "Color-Blind" Society?

Conservative opponents of affirmative action argue that the United States should become a "color-blind" society, in which laws do not recognize race as a deciding factor, and in which private institutions like universities and employers also do not discriminate according to race. In support of the idea of a color-blind society, conservatives frequently quote the Reverend Dr. Martin Luther King, Jr.'s "I have a dream" speech—"I have a dream that my four little children will one day live in a nation where they will not be judged by the color of their skin but by the content of their character."[2] Referring to King's speech, philosophy professor Onkar Ghate writes, "[T]he laudable goal of a color-blind society has been subverted through racial quotas and teachings of multiculturalism. . . . As we commemorate King's

FROM THE BENCH

We are mindful, however, that "[a] core purpose of the Fourteenth Amendment was to do away with all governmentally imposed discrimination based on race." . . . Accordingly, race-conscious admissions policies must be limited in time. This requirement reflects that racial classifications, however compelling their goals, are potentially so dangerous that they may be employed no more broadly than the interest demands. Enshrining a permanent justification for racial preferences would offend this fundamental equal protection principle. We see no reason to exempt race-conscious admissions programs from the requirement that all governmental use of race must have a logical end point. . . .

In the context of higher education, the durational requirement can be met by sunset provisions in race-conscious admissions policies and periodic reviews to determine whether racial preferences are still necessary to achieve student body diversity. Universities in California, Florida, and Washington State, where racial preferences in admissions are prohibited by state law, are currently engaged in experimenting with a wide variety of alternative approaches. Universities in other states can and should draw on the most promising aspects of these race-neutral alternatives as they develop. . . .

The requirement that all race-conscious admissions programs have a termination point "assure[s] all citizens that the deviation from the norm of equal treatment of all racial and ethnic groups is a temporary matter, a measure taken in the service of the goal of equality itself." . . . "It would be a sad day indeed, were America to become a quota-ridden society, with each identifiable minority assigned proportional representation in every desirable walk of life. But that is not the rationale for programs of preferential treatment; the acid test of their justification will be their efficacy in eliminating the need for any racial or ethnic preferences at all."

From *Grutter v. Bollinger*

birth it is depressing to note how far America has deviated from the 'dream.'..."[3]

But supporters of affirmative action vigorously criticize the use of King's words as justification for ending affirmative action, noting that King himself supported such policies. Barbara Miner, editor of an education-reform newspaper, writes, "[U]sing King to argue against affirmative action is profoundly ahistorical. King was fighting against Jim Crow laws in which race was used to deny opportunity and equality. That is far different from affirmative action policies that use race to expand opportunity and make real the rhetoric of equal rights for all."[4]

> • **Is it fair to quote the Reverend Dr. Martin Luther King, Jr.'s speech in opposition to affirmative action?**

The concept of a color-blind society has gained strength primarily as a backlash against the affirmative action programs that originated in the 1960s, but the idea owes much to words written by a U.S. Supreme Court justice more than a century ago. In the infamous *Plessy* v. *Ferguson* decision of 1896, the Court held that racial segregation did not violate the Constitution; only one justice dissented. Justice John Marshall Harlan's words, though originally favoring equal rights for a race of people who had until recently been legally enslaved, are frequently cited by people opposing affirmative action: "Our Constitution is color-blind, and neither knows nor tolerates classes among citizens. In respect of civil rights, all citizens are equal before the law."[5]

However, supporters of affirmative action believe that Harlan's words cannot be taken out of the context in which they were written: a system of public and private discrimination against African Americans in every facet of life. In *Grutter*, a coalition of civil rights groups argued: "This view of color-blindness is legally impoverished because it contradicts the historic purpose and original meaning of the equal protection clause and civil rights laws—to foster genuine equality for groups subordinated under law and by social practice. It also mistakenly presumes that race is an arbitrary concept that has no relevance to the allocation of burdens and benefits in a democratic society. Rather than advancing equality, [this] position perpetuates stark inequalities and deepens social divisions."[6]

The problem with "color-blind" laws, Scott Plous believes, is that they cannot be applied suddenly to a society that has not been color-blind and in which past discrimination has resulted in great inequalities: "Color-blind seniority systems tend to protect white workers against job layoffs, because senior employees are usually white. . . . Likewise, color-blind college admissions favor white students because of their earlier educational advantages."[7]

Many conservatives believe that the only way to achieve color-blindness is to stop classifying people according to race. For example, sociology professor Richard F. Tomasson has advocated dropping questions about race from the U.S. Census, suggesting, "Asking about race is an improper governmental query in a liberal democratic society, one devoted to a color-blind legality and mentality."[8]

In 2003, conservative Californians, already successful in eliminating affirmative action from state university admissions, gained support for a referendum on an amendment to the state's constitution that would make California the nation's first color-blind state. The proposed amendment, officially called the "Classification by Race, Ethnicity, Color, or National Origin Initiative," but frequently referred to as the "Racial Privacy Initiative," prohibits the state, state universities, and local governments from asking questions about people's race or ethnicity and from collecting most data on racial trends. Under such a law, the University of California—already barred from using affirmative action policies—could not ask applicants about their race, and could not even track how many African

Prohibition Against Classifying by Race by State and Other Public Entities

Section 32 is added to Article I of the California Constitution as follows:
Sec. 32

(a) The state shall not classify any individual by race, ethnicity, color or national origin in the operation of public education, public contracting or public employment.

(b) The state shall not classify any individual by race, ethnicity, color or national origin in the operation of any other state operations, unless the legislature specifically determines that said classification serves a compelling state interest and approves said classification by a 2/3 majority in both houses of the legislature, and said classification is subsequently approved by the governor.

(c) For purposes of this section, "classifying" by race, ethnicity, color or national origin shall be defined as the act of separating, sorting or organizing by race, ethnicity, color or national origin including, but not limited to, inquiring, profiling, or collecting such data on government forms....

(f) Otherwise lawful classification of medical research subjects and patients shall be exempt from this section.

(g) Nothing in this section shall prevent law enforcement officers, while carrying out their law enforcement duties, from describing particular persons in otherwise lawful ways. Neither the governor, the legislature nor any statewide agency shall require law enforcement officers to maintain records that track individuals on the basis of said classifications, nor shall the governor, the legislature or any statewide agency withhold funding to law enforcement agencies on the basis of the failure to maintain such records....

(k) For the purposes of this section, "state" shall include, but not necessarily be limited to, the state itself, any city, county, city and county, public university system, including the University of California, California State University, community college district, school district, special district, or any other political subdivision or governmental instrumentality of or within the state.

Source: Classification by Race, Ethnicity, Color, or National Origin Initiative (CRECNO) Qualified for the March 2, 2004, California statewide election.

Americans or Hispanics attended the university. For people who think that "race matters," such a situation is unimaginable, because without being able collect such information, it would be difficult to monitor discrimination. But for people who have grown weary of "reverse discrimination," perhaps eliminating any reference to people's race is the only way to guarantee equality.

• **Does race still "matter"?**

Although the Supreme Court recently upheld affirmative action programs that seek to achieve diversity through individualized consideration, many states are restricting the use of such programs. Several states have enacted "percentage plans" that admit students based on class rank and do not consider race. For some, such steps are not enough, and they would like to see the United States become a "color-blind" nation. However, supporters of affirmative action believe that such policies threaten racial equality.

Affirmative Action and the University of Michigan Cases

1 The Reverend Dr. Martin Luther King, Jr., "I Have a Dream" speech delivered in Washington, D.C. (August 28, 1963). Audio recording and transcript available online at *http://www.americanrhetoric. com/speeches/Ihaveadream.htm.*

2 David Segal, "D.C. Public Interest Firm Puts Affirmative Action on Trial," *Washington Post* (February 20, 1998), p. A1.

3 *NewsHour With Jim Lehrer,* December 22, 1997.

4 *Grutter* v. *Bollinger* (June 23, 2003) (No. 02-241).

5 *Regents of the University of California* v. *Bakke,* 438 US 265 (1978) (Opinion of Powell, J.).

Point: Affirmative Action Is No Longer Justified as a Remedy for Racism

1 *Grutter* v. *Bollinger* (June 23, 2003) (No. 02-241).

2 *Richmond* v. *J.A. Croson Co.,* 488 U.S. 469 (1989).

3 *Adarand Constructors Inc.* v. *Pena,* 515 U.S. 200 (1995) (Scalia, J., concurring in part and concurring in the judgment).

4 Sean Hannity, *Let Freedom Ring: Winning the War of Liberty Over Liberalism.* New York: Regan Books, 2002, pp. 280–282.

5 Larry Elder, *The Ten Things You Can't Say in America.* New York: St. Martin's Press, 2000, pp. 57–58.

6 Ibid., pp. 11–12.

7 Robert Bork, *The Tempting of America: The Political Seduction of the Law.* New York: Touchstone, 1991, p. 106.

8 Terry Eastland, *Ending Affirmative Action: The Case for Colorblind Justice.* New York: Basic Books, 1996, p. 200.

9 Brief for *Amicus Curiae,* Asian American Legal Foundation, *Grutter* v. *Bollinger* (June 23, 2003) (No. 02-241) and *Gratz* v. *Bollinger* (June 23, 2003) (No. 02-516).

10 Brief for *Amicus Curiae,* Claremont Institute Center for Constitutional Jurisprudence, *Grutter* v. *Bollinger* (June 23, 2003) (No. 02-241) and *Gratz* v. *Bollinger* (June 23, 2003) (No. 02-516).

Counterpoint: Racism Still Pervades Society

1 Annie S. Barnes, *Everyday Racism.* Naperville, IL: Sourcebooks, 2000, pp. 55–56.

2 Scott Plous, "Ten Myths About Affirmative Action," *Understanding Prejudice and Discrimination,* ed. Scott Plous. New York: McGraw-Hill, 2002, pp. 206–212.

3 Anna Quindlen, "The Great White Myth," *Debating Affirmative Action: Race, Gender, Ethnicity, and the Politics of Inclusion,* ed. Nicolaus Mills. New York, Delta Books, 1994, p. 212.

4 Charles R. Lawrence III and Mari J. Matsuda, *We Won't Go Back: Making the Case for Affirmative Action.* New York: Houghton Mifflin, 1997, p. 74.

5 Brief for *Amici Curiae,* NAACP Legal Defense and Education Fund Inc. and American Civil Liberties Union, *Grutter* v. *Bollinger* (June 23, 2003) (No. 02-241).

6 Ibid.

7 James Carville, *We're Right, They're Wrong: A Handbook for Spirited Progressives.* New York: Random House, 1996, p. 129.

8 Brief for *Amici Curiae,* United Negro College Fund and Kappa Alpha Psi, *Grutter* v. *Bollinger* (June 23, 2003) (No. 02-241) and *Gratz* v. *Bollinger* (June 23, 2003) (No. 02-516).

9 Annie S. Barnes, *Everyday Racism.* Naperville, IL: Sourcebooks, 2000, p. 88.

10 Brief for *Amicus Curiae,* American Federation of Labor-Congress of Industrial Organizations, *Grutter* v. *Bollinger* (June 23, 2003) (No. 02-241) and *Gratz* v. *Bollinger* (June 23, 2003)

(No. 02-516), citing Marianne Bertrand and Sendhil Mullainathan, "Are Emily and Brendan More Employable Than Lakisha and Jamal?: A Field Experiment on Labor Market Discrimination," unpublished manuscript, University of Chicago School of Business (2002).

11 Brief for *Amicus Curiae*, American Federation of Labor–Congress of Industrial Organizations, *Grutter* v. *Bollinger* (June 23, 2003) (No. 02-241) and *Gratz* v. *Bollinger* (June 23, 2003) (No. 02-516).

12 Brief for *Amici Curiae*, Harvard, Stanford, and Yale Black Law Students Associations, *Grutter* v. *Bollinger* (June 23, 2003) (No. 02-241), citing David B. Rattman and Alan J. Tomkins, *Public Trust and Confidence in the Courts: What Public Opinion Surveys Mean to Judges* (1999).

13 Brief for *Amicus Curiae*, Hispanic National Bar Association, *Grutter* v. *Bollinger* (June 23, 2003) (No. 02-241)

Point: Efforts to Promote "Diversity" Harm Society

1 Terry Eastland, *Ending Affirmative Action: The Case for Colorblind Justice.* New York: Basic Books, 1996, p. 199.

2 Frederick Lynch, preface to *The Diversity Machine: The Drive to Change the "White Male Workplace,"* Rev. ed. New Brunswick, NJ: Transaction Publishers, 2001, p. xxiv.

3 Brief for *Amici Curiae*, Law Professors, *Grutter* v. *Bollinger* (June 23, 2003) (No. 02-241).

4 Richard F. Tomasson, "Affirmative Action in Education," *Affirmative Action: The Pros and Cons of Policy and Practice*, eds. Richard F. Tomasson, Faye J. Crosby, and Sharon D. Herzberger, Rev. ed. Lanham, MD: Rowman & Littlefield Publishers, 2001, p. 194.

5 Dinesh D'Souza, "Sins of Admission," *Debating Affirmative Action: Race, Gender, Ethnicity, and the Politics of Inclusion*, ed. Nicolaus Mills. New York: Delta Books, 1994, p. 232.

6 Richard F. Tomasson, "Affirmative Action in Education," *Affirmative Action: The Pros and Cons of Policy and Practice*, eds. Richard F. Tomasson, Faye J. Crosby, and Sharon D. Herzberger, Rev. ed. Lanham, MD: Rowman & Littlefield Publishers, 2001, p. 195.

7 Dinesh D'Souza, "Sins of Admission," *Debating Affirmative Action: Race, Gender, Ethnicity, and the Politics of Inclusion*, ed. Nicolaus Mills. New York: Delta Books, 1994, p. 232.

Counterpoint: Promoting Diversity Helps Education, Business, and Democracy

1 Brief for *Amici Curiae*, American Educational Research Association, Association of American Colleges and Universities, and American Higher Education Association, *Gratz* v. *Bollinger* (June 23, 2003) (No. 02-516), citing a paper presented by Mitchell Chang at the National Academy of Education Annual Meeting (October 2002).

2 Brief for *Amici Curiae*, American Educational Research Association, Association of American Colleges and Universities, and American Higher Education Association, *Gratz* v. *Bollinger* (June 23, 2003) (No. 02-516), citing a report prepared for the litigation by expert witness Patricia Y. Gurin.

3 Brief for *Amici Curiae*, Harvard, Stanford, and Yale Black Law Students Associations, *Grutter* v. *Bollinger* (June 23, 2003) (No. 02-241).

4 Ibid.

5 Brief for *Amici Curiae*, 65 Leading American Businesses, *Grutter* v. *Bollinger* (June 23, 2003) (No. 02-241) and *Gratz* v. *Bollinger* (June 23, 2003) (No. 02-516).

6 Ibid.

7 Brief for *Amici Curiae*, Media Companies, *Grutter* v. *Bollinger* (June 23, 2003) (No. 02-241) and *Gratz* v. *Bollinger* (June 23, 2003) (No. 02-516).

8 Ibid.

9 Brief for *Amici Curiae*, Hispanic National Bar Association and Hispanic Association of Colleges and Universities, *Grutter* v. *Bollinger* (June 23, 2003) (No. 02-241).

10 Ibid.

11 Brief for *Amicus Curiae*, American Bar Association, *Grutter* v. *Bollinger* (June 23, 2003) (No. 02-241).

Point: Preferences Are Harmful to Recipients and "Nonfavored" Minorities

1 Ruben Navarrette, Jr., "If You Hadn't Been Mexican," *Debating Affirmative Action: Race, Gender, Ethnicity, and the Politics of Inclusion*, ed. Nicolaus Mills. New York: Delta Books, 1994. Originally published in the *Los Angeles Times* (May 12, 1991).

2 *Ho* v. *San Francisco Unified School District*, 59 F. Supp. 2d 1021 (N.D. Cal. 1999).

3 Brief for *Amicus Curiae*, Pacific Legal Foundation, *Gratz* v. *Bollinger* (June 23, 2003) (No. 02-516).

4 Brief for *Amicus Curiae*, Claremont Institute Center for Constitutional Jurisprudence, *Grutter* v. *Bollinger* (June 23, 2003) (No. 02-241) and *Gratz* v. *Bollinger* (June 23, 2003) (No. 02-516).

5 Terry Eastland, *Ending Affirmative Action: The Case for Colorblind Justice.* New York: Basic Books, 1996, p. 198.

6 Larry Elder, *The Ten Things You Can't Say in America.* New York: St. Martin's Press, 2000, pp. 45–46.

7 Richard F. Tomasson, prologue to part two of Richard F. Tomasson, Faye J. Crosby, and Sharon D. Herzberger, *Affirmative Action: The Pros and Cons*

of Policy and Practice, Rev. ed. Lanham, MD: Rowman & Littlefield Publishers, 2001, p. 122.

8 Brief for *Amicus Curiae*, Center for New Black Leadership, *Grutter* v. *Bollinger* (June 23, 2003) (No. 02-241) and *Gratz* v. *Bollinger* (June 23, 2003) (No. 02-516).

9 Charles Murray, "Affirmative Racism," *Debating Affirmative Action: Race, Gender, Ethnicity, and the Politics of Inclusion*, ed. Nicolaus Mills. New York: Delta Books, 1994, pp. 200–202.

10 Robert Bork, *The Tempting of America: The Political Seduction of the Law.* New York: Touchstone, 1991, p. 107.

11 Dinesh D'Souza, "Sins of Admission," *Debating Affirmative Action: Race, Gender, Ethnicity, and the Politics of Inclusion*, ed. Nicolaus Mills. New York: Delta Books, 1994, p. 232.

12 Brief for *Amicus Curiae*, Asian American Legal Foundation, *Grutter* v. *Bollinger* (June 23, 2003) (No. 02-241) and *Gratz* v. *Bollinger* (June 23, 2003) (No. 02-516).

13 *Grutter* v. *Bollinger* (June 23, 2003) (No. 02-241) (Thomas, J., dissenting).

Counterpoint: Affirmative Action Policies Help People for Whom the Playing Field Is Not Level

1 Tanya Barrientos, "Unconventional Wisdom: A Success Story Fit to Print," *Philadelphia Inquirer*, May 17, 2003.

2 Scott Plous, "Ten Myths About Affirmative Action." Available online at *http://www.socialpsychology.org/pdf/jsi96.pdf.*

3 Faye J. Crosby and Sharon D. Herzberger, "The Effectiveness of Affirmative Action," *Affirmative Action: The Pros and Cons of Policy and Practice*, eds. Richard F. Tomasson, Faye J. Crosby, and Sharon D. Herzberger, Rev. ed. Lanham, MD: Rowman & Littlefield Publishers, 2001, p. 64.

4 Ibid.

5 Kim Gandy, "Save Affirmative Action," *National NOW Times* (Spring 2003). Available online at *http://www.now.org/spring-2003/viewpoint.html*.

6 Brief for *Amici Curiae*, Members of Congress, *Gratz* v. *Bollinger* (June 23, 2003) (No. 02-516).

7 Brief for *Amici Curiae*, NAACP Legal Defense and Education Fund Inc. and American Civil Liberties Union, *Grutter* v. *Bollinger* (June 23, 2003) (No. 02-241).

8 Scott Plous, "Ten Myths About Affirmative Action," *Understanding Prejudice and Discrimination*, ed. Scott Plous. New York: McGraw-Hill, 2003, pp. 206–212.

9 *Gratz* v. *Bollinger* (June 23, 2003) (No. 02-516).

Conclusion: The Future of Affirmative Action

1 Brief for *Amici Curiae*, Members of Congress, *Gratz* v. *Bollinger* (June 23, 2003) (No. 02-516).

2 The Reverend Dr. Martin Luther King, Jr., "I Have a Dream," speech delivered in Washington, D.C. (August 28, 1963). Audio recording and transcript available online at *http://www.americanrhetoric.com/speeches/Ihaveadream.htm*.

3 Onkar Ghate, "The Destruction of Martin Luther King's Dream of a Colorblind Society," *Capitalism Magazine* (January 15, 2001). Available online at *http://www.capmag.com/article.asp?ID=119*. See also Sean Hannity, *Let Freedom Ring: Winning the War of Liberty Over Liberalism*. New York: Regan Books, 2002, p. 235.

4 Barbara Miner, "Conservatives Exploit King to Promote 'Colorblind' Politics," *Rethinking Schools Online* 17 no. 4 (Summer 2003). Available online at *http://rethinkingschools.com/archive/17_04/colo174.shtml*.

5 Brief for *Amicus Curiae*, Claremont Institute Center for Constitutional Jurisprudence, *Grutter* v. *Bollinger* (June 23, 2003) (No. 02-241) and *Gratz* v. *Bollinger* (June 23, 2003) (No. 02-516), citing *Plessy* v. *Ferguson*, 163 U.S. 537 (1896) (Harlan, J., dissenting).

6 Brief for *Amici Curiae*, Coalition for Economic Equity, Santa Clara University School of Law Center for Social Justice and Public Service, Charles Houston Bar Association, and California Association of Black Lawyers, *Grutter* v. *Bollinger* (June 23, 2003) (No. 02-241).

7 Scott Plous, "Ten Myths About Affirmative Action," *Understanding Prejudice and Discrimination*, ed. Scott Plous. New York: McGraw-Hill, 2003, pp. 206–212.

8 Richard F. Tomasson, "Affirmative Action for Whom," *Affirmative Action: The Pros and Cons of Policy and Practice*, eds. Richard F. Tomasson, Faye J. Crosby, and Sharon D. Herzberger, Rev. ed. Lanham, MD: Rowman & Littlefield Publishers, 2001, p. 184.

General Resources

Mills, Nicolaus, ed. *Debating Affirmative Action: Race, Gender, Ethnicity, and the Politics of Inclusion.* Delta Books, 1994.

Tomasson, Richard F., Faye J. Crosby, and Sharon D. Herzberger. *Affirmative Action: The Pros and Cons of Policy and Practice,* Rev. Ed. Rowman & Littlefield Publishers, 2001.

Opposing Affirmative Action
Books

Bork, Robert H. *The Tempting of America: The Political Seduction of the Law.* Touchstone, 1990.

Eastland, Terry. *Ending Affirmative Action: The Case for Colorblind Justice.* Basic Books, 1996.

Elder, Larry. *The Ten Things You Can't Say in America.* St. Martin's Press, 2000.

Hannity, Sean. *Let Freedom Ring: Winning the War of Liberty Over Liberalism.* Regan Books, 2002.

Lynch, Frederick R. *The Diversity Machine: The Drive to Change the "White Male Workplace,"* Rev. Ed. Transaction Publishers, 2001.

Websites
Cato Institute

www.cato.org

Libertarian think-tank offering extensive information about affirmative action and many other topics related to government regulation of individual liberties.

Claremont Institute

www.claremont.org

Think-tank and public interest law firm offering conservative viewpoints on constitutional civil-liberties issues.

Pacific Legal Foundation

www.pacificlegal.org

California-based conservative public interest law firm, especially interested in enforcing Proposition 209, California's affirmative action ban.

Favoring Affirmative Action
Books

Ancheta, Angelo. *Revisiting* Bakke *and Diversity-Based Admissions: Constitutional Law, Social Science Research, and the University of Michigan Affirmative Action Cases.* The Civil Rights Project at Harvard University, 2003.

Barnes, Annie S. *Everyday Racism.* Sourcebooks, 2000.

Carville, James. *We're Right, They're Wrong: A Handbook for Spirited Progressives.* Random House, 1996.

Lawrence, Charles R. III, and Mari J. Matsuda. *We Won't Go Back: Making the Case for Affirmative Action.* Houghton Mifflin, 1997.

Websites

American Civil Liberties Union

www.aclu.org

Organization dedicated to protecting individual civil liberties, including the rights of the accused, freedom of speech, and freedom from discrimination.

American Educational Research Association

www.aera.net

Organization devoted to research on educational topics and a strong supporter of affirmative action.

The Civil Rights Project, Harvard University

www.civilrightsproject.harvard.edu

Extensive information about the benefits of diversity in higher education.

National Association for the Advancement of Colored People

www.naacp.org

Advocacy organization concentrating on enforcing civil rights and improving living conditions.

United Negro College Fund

www.uncf.org

Association of historically black colleges and universities.

Legislation and Case Law

University of California Regents v. Bakke, 438 U.S. 265 (1978)
Invalidated University of Califonia's medical school admission policy reserving a set number of places for minority students. However, writing alone, Justice Lewis Powell stated that diversity could serve as a legitimate rationale for affirmative action policies that do not apply strict quotas.

California Civil Rights Initiative, Constitution of the State of California, Article I § 31.
Adopted in 1996 as "Proposition 209," stating: "The state shall not discriminate against, or grant preferential treatment to, any individual or group on the basis of race, sex, color, ethnicity, or national origin in the operation of public employment, public education, or public contracting."

Hopwood v. Texas, 78 F.3d 932 (5th Cir. 1996)
Held that the Constitution prohibits the consideration of race in university admissions. Overruled by *Gratz* v. *Bollinger*.

The Texas "10 Percent Plan," Texas Education Code Sec. 51.803
Adopted in 1997, guarantees admission to Texas' public universities to each student finishing in the top 10 percent of his or her Texas high school class.

The "One Florida" Plan, Florida Administrative Code Sec. 6C-6.002
Adopted in 2000, guarantees admission to one of Florida's public universities to each student finishing in the top 20 percent of his or her Florida high school class.

Gratz v. Bollinger (No. 02-516) (June 23, 2003)
Struck down the University of Michigan's college admission policy, which automatically awarded minority applicants 20 points on a scale of 150.

Grutter v. Bollinger (No. 02-241) (June 23, 2003)
Upheld the University of Michigan's law school admission policy, which considered race alongside other factors and sought to enroll a "critical mass" of minority students.

Concepts and Standards

affirmative action

color-blind

equal protection

underrepresented minorities

disadvantaged minorities

reverse discrimination

quota system

diversity

critical mass

societal discrimination

creditor or debtor race

victicrat mentality

preferential treatment

economic injustice

segregation

equal opportunity

equal access to justice

misplacement

selective admission

internal stigma

external stigma

capping out

glass ceiling

trickle-down

percentage plans

Beginning Legal Research

The goal of Point/Counterpoint is not only to provide the reader with an introduction to a controversial issue affecting society, but also to encourage the reader to explore the issue more fully. This appendix, then, is meant to serve as a guide to the reader in researching the current state of the law as well as exploring some of the public-policy arguments as to why existing laws should be changed or new laws are needed.

Like many types of research, legal research has become much faster and more accessible with the invention of the Internet. This appendix discusses some of the best starting points, but of course "surfing the Net" will uncover endless additional sources of information—some more reliable than others. Some important sources of law are not yet available on the Internet, but these can generally be found at the larger public and university libraries. Librarians usually are happy to point patrons in the right direction.

The most important source of law in the United States is the Constitution. Originally enacted in 1787, the Constitution outlines the structure of our federal government and sets limits on the types of laws that the federal government and state governments can pass. Through the centuries, a number of amendments have been added to or changed in the Constitution, most notably the first ten amendments, known collectively as the Bill of Rights, which guarantee important civil liberties. Each state also has its own constitution, many of which are similar to the U.S. Constitution. It is important to be familiar with the U.S. Constitution because so many of our laws are affected by its requirements. State constitutions often provide protections of individual rights that are even stronger than those set forth in the U.S. Constitution.

Within the guidelines of the U.S. Constitution, Congress—both the House of Representatives and the Senate—passes bills that are either vetoed or signed into law by the President. After the passage of the law, it becomes part of the United States Code, which is the official compilation of federal laws. The state legislatures use a similar process, in which bills become law when signed by the state's governor. Each state has its own official set of laws, some of which are published by the state and some of which are published by commercial publishers. The U.S. Code and the state codes are an important source of legal research; generally, legislators make efforts to make the language of the law as clear as possible.

However, reading the text of a federal or state law generally provides only part of the picture. In the American system of government, after the legislature passes laws and the executive (U.S. President or state governor) signs them, it is up to the judicial branch of the government, the court system, to interpret the laws and decide whether they violate any provision of the Constitution. At the state level, each state's supreme court has the ultimate authority in determining what a law means and whether or not it violates the state constitution. However, the federal courts—headed by the U.S. Supreme Court—can review state laws and court decisions to determine whether they violate federal laws or the U.S. Constitution. For example, a state court may find that a particular criminal law is valid under the state's constitution, but a federal court may then review the state court's decision and determine that the law is invalid under the U.S. Constitution.

It is important, then, to read court decisions when doing legal research. The Constitution uses language that is intentionally very general—for example, prohibiting "unreasonable searches and seizures" by the police—and court cases often provide more guidance. For example, the U.S. Supreme Court's 2001 decision in *Kyllo* v. *United States* held that scanning the outside of a person's house using a heat sensor to determine whether the person is growing marijuana is unreasonable—*if* it is done without a search warrant secured from a judge. Supreme Court decisions provide the most definitive explanation of the law of the land, and it is therefore important to include these in research. Often, when the Supreme Court has not decided a case on a particular issue, a decision by a federal appeals court or a state supreme court can provide guidance; but just as laws and constitutions can vary from state to state, so can federal courts be split on a particular interpretation of federal law or the U.S. Constitution. For example, federal appeals courts in Louisiana and California may reach opposite conclusions in similar cases.

Lawyers and courts refer to statutes and court decisions through a formal system of citations. Use of these citations reveals which court made the decision (or which legislature passed the statute) and when and enables the reader to locate the statute or court case quickly in a law library. For example, the legendary Supreme Court case *Brown* v. *Board of Education* has the legal citation 347 U.S. 483 (1954). At a law library, this 1954 decision can be found on page 483 of volume 347 of the U.S. Reports, the official collection of the Supreme Court's decisions. Citations can also be helpful in locating court cases on the Internet.

Understanding the current state of the law leads only to a partial under-standing of the issues covered by the POINT/COUNTERPOINT series. For a fuller understanding of the issues, it is necessary to look at public-policy arguments that the current state of the law is not adequately addressing the issue. Many groups lobby for new legislation or changes to existing legislation; the National Rifle Association (NRA), for example, lobbies Congress and the state legislatures constantly to make existing gun control laws less restrictive and not to pass additional laws. The NRA and other groups dedicated to various causes might also intervene in pending court cases: a group such as Planned Parenthood might file a brief *amicus curiae* (as "a friend of the court")—called an "amicus brief"—in a lawsuit that could affect abortion rights. Interest groups also use the media to influence public opinion, issuing press releases and frequently appearing in interviews on news programs and talk shows. The books in POINT/COUNTERPOINT list some of the interest groups that are active in the issue at hand, but in each case there are countless other groups working at the local, state, and national levels. It is important to read everything with a critical eye, for sometimes interest groups present information in a way that can be read only to their advantage. The informed reader must always look for bias.

Finding sources of legal information on the Internet is relatively simple thanks to "portal" sites such as FindLaw (*www.findlaw.com*), which provides access to a variety of constitutions, statutes, court opinions, law review articles, news articles, and other resources—including all Supreme Court decisions issued since 1893. Other useful sources of information include the U.S. Government Printing Office (*www.gpo.gov*), which contains a complete copy of the U.S. Code, and the Library of Congress's THOMAS system (*thomas.loc.gov*), which offers access to bills pending before Congress as well as recently passed laws. Of course, the Internet changes every second of every day, so it is best to do some independent searching. Most cases, studies, and opinions that are cited or referred to in public debate can be found online—and *everything* can be found in one library or another.

The Internet can provide a basic understanding of most important legal issues, but not all sources can be found there. To find some documents it is necessary to visit the law library of a university or a public law library; some cities have public law libraries, and many library systems keep legal documents at the main branch. On the following page are some common citation forms.

////////

COMMON CITATION FORMS

Source of Law	Sample Citation	Notes
U.S. Supreme Court	*Employment Division* v. *Smith*, 485 U.S. 660 (1988)	The U.S. Reports is the official record of Supreme Court decisions. There is also an unofficial Supreme Court ("S.Ct.") reporter.
U.S. Court of Appeals	*United States* v. *Lambert*, 695 F.2d 536 (11th Cir.1983)	Appellate cases appear in the Federal Reporter, designated by "F." The 11th Circuit has jurisdiction in Alabama, Florida, and Georgia.
U.S. District Court	*Carillon Importers, Ltd.* v. *Frank Pesce Group, Inc.*, 913 F.Supp. 1559 (S.D.Fla.1996)	Federal trial-level decisions are reported in the Federal Supplement ("F.Supp."). Some states have multiple federal districts; this case originated in the Southern District of Florida.
U.S. Code	Thomas Jefferson Commemoration Commission Act, 36 U.S.C., §149 (2002)	Sometimes the popular names of legislation—names with which the public may be familiar—are included with the U.S. Code citation.
State Supreme Court	*Sterling* v. *Cupp*, 290 Ore. 611, 614, 625 P.2d 123, 126 (1981)	The Oregon Supreme Court decision is reported in both the state's reporter and the Pacific regional reporter.
State statute	Pennsylvania Abortion Control Act of 1982, 18 Pa. Cons. Stat. 3203-3220 (1990)	States use many different citation formats for their statutes.

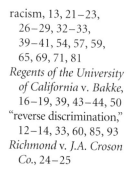

page:
17: Associated Press/AP
57: Associated Press/AP
78: © Reprinted with special permission of North America Syndicate

ALAN MARZILLI, of Durham, North Carolina, is an independent consultant working on several ongoing projects for state and federal government agencies and nonprofit organizations. He has spoken about mental health issues in more than twenty-five states, the District of Columbia, and Puerto Rico; his work includes training mental health administrators, nonprofit management and staff, and people with mental illness and their family members on a wide variety of topics, including effective advocacy, community-based mental health services, and housing. He has written several handbooks and training curricula that are used nationally. He managed statewide and national mental health advocacy programs and worked for several public interest lobbying organizations in Washington, D.C., while studying law at Georgetown University.